Windows 10 Explained

by

N. Kantaris

Bernard Babani (publishing) Ltd
The Grampians
Shepherds Bush Road
London W6 7NF
England

www.babanibooks.com

Please Note

Although every care has been taken with the production of this book to ensure that all information is correct at the time of writing and that any projects, designs, modifications and/or programs, etc., contained herewith, operate in a correct and safe manner and also that any components specified are normally available in Great Britain, the Publishers and Author(s) do not accept responsibility in any way for the failure (including fault in design) of any project, design, modification or program to work correctly or to cause damage to any equipment that it may be connected to or used in conjunction with, or in respect of any other damage or injury that may be so caused, nor do the Publishers accept responsibility in any way for the failure to obtain specified components.

Notice is also given that if equipment that is still under warranty is modified in any way or used or connected with home-built equipment then that warranty may be void.

© 2015 BERNARD BABANI (publishing) LTD

First Published - October 2015

British Library Cataloguing in Publication Data:

A catalogue record for this book is available from the British Library

ISBN 978 0 85934 757 0

Cover Design by Gregor Arthur

Printed and bound in Great Britain for Bernard Babani (publishing) Ltd

About this Book

Windows 10 Explained was written so that you can explore quickly the workings of Microsoft's Windows latest OS (Operating System).

Windows 10 comes as a free upgrade to all versions of Windows from Windows 7 through to Windows 8.1. To see if your PC, laptop or tablet is capable of running the new OS, use the **Get Windows 10** App which is to be found on your desktop's **Task bar** (the first icon on the left shown below).

 If this icon is not on your device, you need to go to **Control Panel** and use the **Windows Update** option shown to the right and install all the updates offered. Once this is done, the **Get Windows 10** App will appear on your device's **Task bar**.

Finally, left-clicking or tapping the **Get Windows 10** App icon, displays the screen shown below.

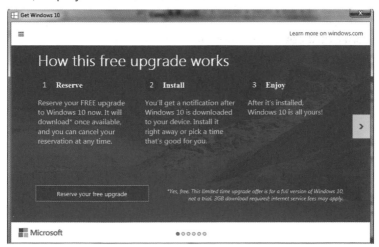

This is the first of several screens that you access by clicking/tapping on the arrow icon on the right of the screen.

Note the **Menu** icon ≡ at the top-left of the screen. Clicking or tapping this icon, opens the menu options shown overleaf.

Amongst the various menu options, listed, you should first select the **Check your PC** (pointed to here on the left).

Tapping or clicking this entry, opens a screen similar to the one displayed below for a laptop running Windows 8.1. Obviously, in your case what is displayed depends on which version of Windows you are using and what hardware or software is included.

> **Note:** Windows 10 will remove **Windows Media Center** as it does not support it anymore.

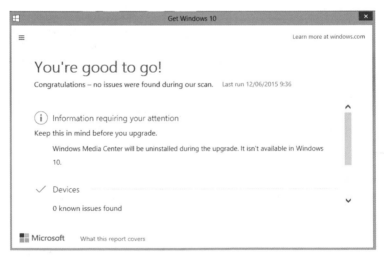

If everything looks 'good', then you are ready to download and install your Windows upgrade. If not, you will be told what you have to do so as to be able to run Windows 10 on your device.

There are chapters that include the following:

- An overview of the Start menu options, Desktop, Taskbar, the Tray Notification Area, running Apps, creating User Accounts, managing Windows Settings and Personalising your PC.

- How to use the Cortana personal assistant, the new Edge browser, the Desktop File Explorer, OneDrive, Internet Explorer and how to practice with the e-mail App and use the People App and Calendar.

- How to work with and organise your digital photo-graphs and import them from your camera or scanner, use the Photo App, the Groove Music App and the Media Player to store and play your music and burn CDs.

- How to use the Maps App and the Bing maps, search for locations and see them in Road, Bird's Eye and Streetside views and get driving directions.

- How to connect to wireless networks and set up a Home Group, share a printer and network PCs. How to use mobility tools to keep your laptop running while away from home.

- How to use Accessibility features if you have problems using the keyboard or mouse or have poor eyesight, how to keep your PC healthy and backup your important files.

The material in this book is presented using everyday language, avoiding jargon as much as possible. It was written with a non-technical, non-computer literate person in mind.

I hope that with the help of this book, you will be able to get the most out of your tablet, laptop and desktop computer when using Windows 10, and that you will be able to do it in the shortest, most effective and enjoyable way. But most of all, have fun!

About the Author

Noel Kantaris graduated in Electrical Engineering at Bristol University and after spending three years in the Electronics Industry in London, took up a Tutorship in Physics at the University of Queensland. Research interests in Ionospheric Physics, led to the degrees of M.E. in Electronics and Ph.D. in Physics. On return to the UK, he took up a Post-Doctoral Research Fellowship in Radio Physics at the University of Leicester, and then a lecturing position in Engineering at the Camborne School of Mines, Cornwall, (part of Exeter University), where he was also the CSM Computing Manager. Lately he also served as IT Director of FFC Ltd.

Trademarks

Microsoft, **Windows 10**, **Windows 8.1**, **Windows 8**, **Windows 7**, are either registered trademarks or trademarks of Microsoft Corporation.

Wi-Fi is a trademark of the Wi-Fi Alliance.

All other brand and product names used in the book are recognised as trademarks, or registered trademarks, of their respective companies.

Contents

1

Installing Windows 10

Upgrading to Windows 10

There are two ways of upgrading to Windows 10. One method is to wait for the Windows 10 App notification to appear, while the second is to download the Windows 10 Media Creator Tool and carry on from there.

When you receive the Windows 10 App notification shown in Fig. 1.1, you are ready to begin the upgrade by clicking or tapping the **Restart now** button.

However, the very act of capturing this screen, caused the removal of the notification App from my PC! This left me with only two choices:

Fig. 1.1 The Windows 10 Notification Update.

(i) either wait for the notification to reappear sometime in the future (a bit like *Waiting for Godo*) or

(ii) select the second method of upgrading, particularly as I was informed by a friend of problems in upgrading using the App notification – It started well, but froze shortly afterwards!

However, if you haven't applied to Microsoft for reservation of the upgrade via the App notification method and you are about to use the suggested second method of upgrading, then perhaps you need to know what is the minimum system requirements. On the other hand, if your present system runs Windows 8.1 successfully, then you can skip the next section.

System Requirements

To run Windows 10 a PC requires at least:

- A processor with a speed of 1 GHz or faster with 1 GB (gigabyte) for a 32-bit (x86) system or 2 GB for a 64-bit (x64) system of available RAM.

- A graphics card that is DirectX 9 compatible with a WDDM 1.0 or higher driver and a minimum screen resolution of 1024 x 768.

- 20 GB of available hard disc space.

- Access to the Internet to get mail or download and run Apps from Windows Apps Store.

- To use Windows Touch, you need a Tablet with an ARM processor or a monitor that supports multi-touch.

- Depending on resolution, video playback may require additional memory and advanced graphics hardware.

- HomeGroup requires a network and PCs running either Windows 7, 8, 8.1 or Windows 10.

Downloading and installing the Windows 10 free upgrade might take more than two hours, depending on the speed of your network and on the version of Windows (7, 8 or 8.1) you have installed. You have about 3.5 GB to download and the speed at which this is achieved also depends on whether or not you have disabled your firewall for the period and your broadband is fast enough and stable. Then follows the installation itself with numerous checks on compatibility, gathering information, installing, 'doing more things', including a number of restarts, so be very patient and have a jug of coffee near you!

Upgrading Via Windows 10 Media Creation Tool

To download the Windows 10 Media Creation tool, go to:

http://www.microsoft.com/en-us/software-downlowad/windows10

A screen similar to that in Fig. 1.2 (you will have to scroll down a bit) will then display on your screen.

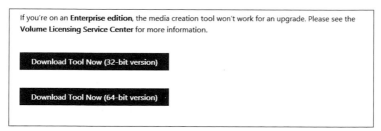

Fig. 1.2 Getting the Windows 10 Media Creation Tool.

Note: This procedure does not work with the **Windows Enterprise edition**.

Select to download the 32-bit or the 64-bit version of the Tool, depending on which system computer you have - to find out go to **Start**, **Control Panel**, then select **System** and look at the **System type**. It will tell you whether you system is a 64-bit or 32-bit.

Having selected which tool to download, click **Run** on the displayed screen, which displays the **Windows 10 Setup** screen, as shown below.

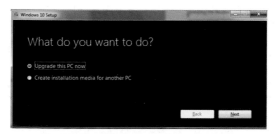

Fig. 1.3 The Windows 10 Setup Screen.

Clicking or tapping **Upgrade this PC now**, starts the download action and after 15 minutes or so, it first **Verifies** the download, then displays a succession of screens, such as **Creating Windows Media**, **Windows Preparation**, **Getting Updates** and **Licence terms**.

Selecting the **Accept** button on the **Licence terms** screen, displays further information on **Getting Updates** and **Making sure you're ready to install**, before displaying the screen in Fig. 1.4, telling you that **Windows media** (if installed on your PC) is not supported by Windows 10 and will be removed.

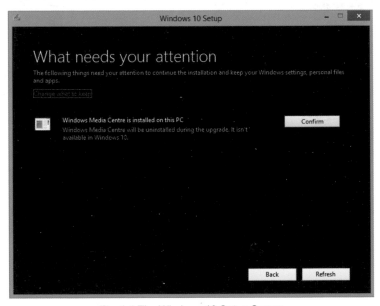

Fig. 1.4 The Windows 10 Setup Screen.

Selecting the **Confirm** button, the **Ready to Install** screen is displayed, as shown in Fig. 1.5 on the next page. This is your last chance to abort the Windows 10 installation!

If your current Windows installation is a **Professional** version, **Windows 10 Pro** is installed, while if it is a **Home** version, **Windows 10 Home** will be installed. On this screen, you can also choose to **Keep personal files and apps** or **Change what to keep**.

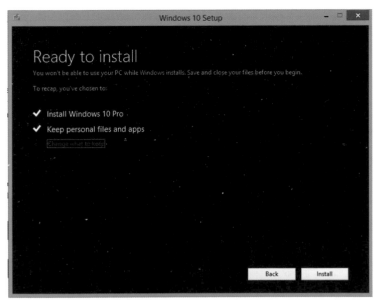

Fig. 1.5 The Ready to Install Screen.

Selecting to **Install**, starts the process. Ten minutes later and just over an hour from downloading the **Windows 10 Media Creation Tool**, the **Upgrading Windows** process starts in earnest, as shown in Fig. 1.6 below.

As you can see, you are constantly informed, in percentage terms, how far the installation process is in. At least an other hour later, including a few restarts, the **Hello welcome back** screen appears.

Fig. 1.6 The Upgrading Windows Screen.

Selecting the **Next** button, displays a screen informing you that you can **Use Express settings** for now, as you can change these later, if you so wish.

The next screen gives you information on the new **Apps**, such as **Photos, Music, Microsoft Edge** and **Films & TV**. Selecting **Next**, you are asked to sign in with your Windows Password. Finally and after signing in, two more screens are displayed, the first to let you know that the procedure of **Taking care of a few things** has started, followed by the **Setting up your apps** initiation.

> **Note:** You are warned not to turn off your PC while these procedures are taking place!

After further 15 minutes, the **Start** screen appears, as shown below in Fig. 1.7. It has taken only 2 hours and 15 minutes from start to finish!

Fig. 1.7 The Start Screen.

As I said earlier, the time taken depends on the speed of your network and on the version of Windows you started with. The speed of the download also depends on whether or not you have disable your firewall for the period.

Touching any key on the keyboard or swiping upwards on a touch sensitive screen, opens up the **Sign in** screen, as shown in Fig. 1.8 below.

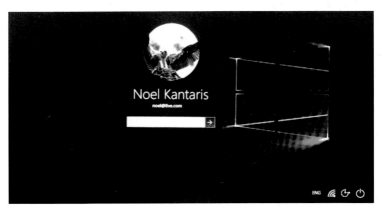

Fig. 1.8 The Sign In Screen.

After signing in, your **Desktop** screen appears, as shown below in Fig. 1.9 for my laptop with the **Start** button activated.

Fig. 1.9 The Desktop Screen.

> **Note:** If you are new to Windows 10 and you have just upgraded, say, from Windows 7 or you've just bought a new PC running Windows 10, you might at first be puzzled not knowing how to configure your computer or change screens, but don't worry, all will be explained in good time! The rest of this chapter only deals with what security is required to keep your computer safe, how to fix a mailing bug in Office Outlook and what is new in Windows 10.

Internet Security

By default, Windows 10 provides security on the Internet using the Windows **Defender** App which includes its anti-virus, anti-spyware and **Firewall**.

With Windows **Defender**, your computer can be made very secure with its protection working unobtrusively in the background, However, although Microsoft claims that the Windows **Defender** App offers absolute protection, studies have found that third party anti-virus programs still offer better protection. I leave that to you, but don't run more that one such programan on your computer, as you will get conflicts as a result.

Fixing a Bug in Office Outlook

A lot of people might have been using the Microsoft Office Outlook program for e-mail messaging, keeping their contacts and calendar events, prior to upgrading to Windows 10. If you are anything like me, the first thing you would do, after installing Windows 10, is to check your e-mail messages in Office Outlook and answer a few.

> **Note:** If you are not using Office Outlook, skip the rest of this section. E-mail configuration and use will be discussed at a later chapter.

I have been using Office Outlook 2013 and its predecessors for several years now, so you can imagine my surprise on starting the program to be told that I was not connected to the Internet especially since I had just been using it for the upgrade! It took me sometime to figure out what was happening!

It transpired that, in my particular case at least, Windows 10 removed my Website-based e-mail account and only kept my live.com account So, no wonder Outlook could not connect to the Internet. Having recreated my e-mail account, e-mail messages started purring in. Then, another surprise:

All sent messages, just sat in the Outbox and stayed there!

As it turned out, I was not the only one experiencing this problem. The best suggestion was that some Office Outlook files were missing or corrupted during the upgrade to Windows 10. To rectify this, a scan of the computer was needed. To achieve this, either right-click or touch and hold the **Start** button on the extreme bottom-left of the screen, also shown here, to open the menu shown in Fig. 1.10 below. :

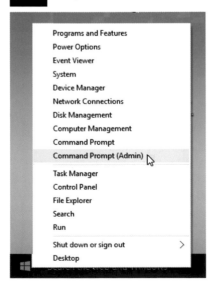

Next, click or tap the **Command Prompt (Admin)** entry to open a screen similar to that shown in Fig. 1.11 on the next page.

Fig. 1.10 The Start Button Menu.

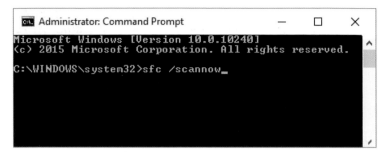

Fig. 1.11 The Administrator's Command Prompt with Typed Command.

The actual command typed at the prompt is:

`Sfc /scannow`

which stands for 'System File Checker'. The 'scannow' option scans and repairs important Windows system files - the space between command and its option is important. Pressing the **Enter** key, starts the process which takes several minutes to complete. It then confirms that it has found some corrupt files and has repaired them. Once this is done, you must reboot your computer by restarting it which fixes the Outlook problem.

What is New in Windows 10

Microsoft have really taken on board criticisms and concerns voiced by users. As a result, Windows 10 embodies the best of Windows 7 and Windows 8.1 in the dual functionality of the **Start** button, and with many new features.

(1) The **Start** button:

(a) Tap and hold or right-click the **Start** button, shown here, to open a list of options shown in Fig. 1.10 on page 9. This makes the access to the various areas listed a lot easier to get to than in previous versions of Windows.

(b) Tap or left-click the **Start** button to open the two-column **Start** menu shown in Fig. 1.9 on page 7.

The left column of the **Start** menu allows access to **All Apps**, **Power options**, **Settings** and **File Explorer**, as well as most used Apps by simply tapping or clicking the entries, while the right column displays tiled icons that, when tapped or clicked, open the selected App. To see more such Apps, either swipe upwards or scroll down.

(2) Cortana: The personal digital assistant that can be used to search the Web or used to transcribe and send an e-mail, purely through voice commands. It is a cross between Apple's **Siri** and **Google Now**, but with some added functionality. It started life as the **Windows Phone** assistant.

To activate **Cortana**, tap or click the **Search the web and Windows** area on the **Task** bar, immediately to the right of the **Start** button, which displays the screen in Fig. 1.12.

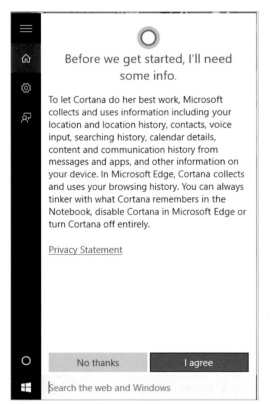

As you can see, **Cortana** requires your permission to search your PC for information, including your location. Tap or click **I agree** to continue.

Before we get started, I'll need some info.

To let Cortana do her best work, Microsoft collects and uses information including your location and location history, contacts, voice input, searching history, calendar details, content and communication history from messages and apps, and other information on your device. In Microsoft Edge, Cortana collects and uses your browsing history. You can always tinker with what Cortana remembers in the Notebook, disable Cortana in Microsoft Edge or turn Cortana off entirely.

Privacy Statement

No thanks   I agree

Search the web and Windows

Fig. 1.12 Cortana in Action.

Cortana then asks you by what name she should call you, followed by a request to repeat a phrase so she can get used to your voice. From then on, you can tap or click on the microphone and make a request, as shown here in Fig. 1.13.

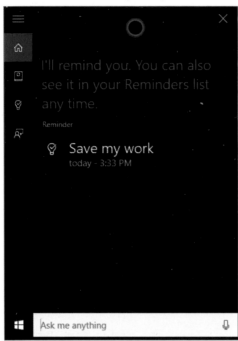

Try this feature, it is great fun. You can use it to ask any questions, but you might not always get the right answer!

Fig. 1.13 Performing a Request.

(3) Microsoft Edge: This is the new Internet browser in Windows 10, its tile shown on the left (although **Internet Explorer** is still there in the tiled Apps column of the **Start** menu, shown on the right). The latter is retained as it supports specific legacy plug-ins that are not supported by Edge.

Microsoft Edge allows you to write comments (using a mouse, a finger or a special pen) on touch sensitive screens, as shown in Fig. 1.14 on the next page. You can also use a highlighter or even the keyboard to type your thoughts, before sharing these with your friends!

You can choose to **Clip** a Web page, **Collapse** a typed message and/or save it. Tapping of clicking the **Exit** option at the top-right of the screen, removes all comments and returns the Web page in its original display.

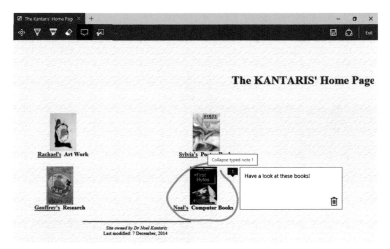

Fig. 1.14 Example of Web Page with Doodle and Typed Message.

Perhaps the inclusion of **Cortana** in **Microsoft Edge** is worth exploring, but don't expect exact results. Try it and expect to be surprised!

(4) The Task Viewer: This is an icon on the **Task** bar (the first to the right of **Cortana**'s microphone), shown here to the left, that you tap or click to view all running tasks, as shown in Fig. 1.15. You can achieve the same thing by using the key combination **Alt+Tab** – hold down the **Alt** key and tap the **Tab** key.

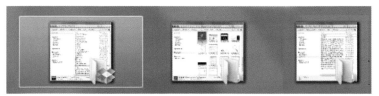

Fig. 1.15 Viewing Running Tasks..

It is easy to switch from one running task to another by simply pointing and tapping or clicking.

(5) Snap Assist: You can now use all four corners of your screen to display four running Apps simultaneously (instead of only two in previous versions of Windows), each taking one quarter of the screen, as shown in Fig. 1.16.

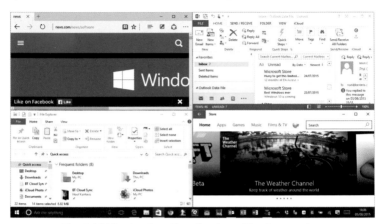

Fig. 1.16 Viewing Four Running Apps Simultaneously .

While you snap the first running App into one corner, the unused part of the screen displays the remaining running Apps as thump nails, making it easier for you to pick the next.

(6) The Action Centre: To display the **Action Centre**, tap or

click its icon on the **Task** bar, pointed to in Fig. 1.17. It provides notification from various Apps (none shown here) and also various settings buttons at the lower half of the screen for easy access.

Fig. 1.17 The Action Centre.

(7) Universal Apps: Windows 10 has a new **Windows Store**, as shown in Fig. 1.18, where you can download

Fig. 1.18 The Action Centre.

programs or modern Apps, many of which are universal, meaning they will run on your PC as well as on your Windows tablet or phone. The interface of such Apps changes to suit the different screen sizes. This allows you to access your e-mail messages or Calendar using different Windows devices.

Turning Off Your Computer

There are two alternative methods of turning off your computer. These are:

(a) Tap or click the **Start** button, then tap or click the **Power**

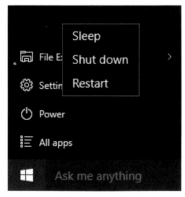

Fig. 1.19 The Lower Part of the Start Menu.

button on the displayed **Start** menu (only the bottom half of the menu is shown in Fig. 1.19). This opens a sub-menu with a list of three options.

   Sleep puts your computer in **Sleep** mode which means that the PC turns off, but uses very low power to keep all programs and Apps running so they are instantly available to you when you re-awake your PC by pressing the power button.

Shut down closes all programs and Apps, while **Restart** closes all programs and Apps, turns off your PC, then turns it on again. The last two options clear the PC's memory and any work not saved, prior to taking such action, is lost. I suggest you put your PC into **Sleep** mode for the present.

(b) Touch and hold or right-click the **Start** button to open the alternative **Start** menu (only the bottom half of the menu is shown in Fig. 1.20), then tap or click the **Shut down or sign out** option. This displays a sub-menu with four options, as shown below.

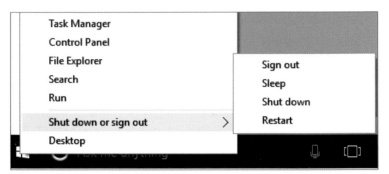

Fig. 1.20 The Lower Part of the Alternative Start Menu.

As you can see, there is only one extra option on the displayed sub-menu, namely, **Sign out**. This allows a user to sign off the PC, allowing another member of the family to take over the PC (by signing in), without compromising the previous user's settings and data - more about this later.

For the time being, I suggest you select to put your PC in **Sleep** mode, so you are ready to restart it after some well earned break!

2

The Windows Environment

The Windows 10 Screens

When you restart your computer, the **Start** screen, shown in Fig. 1.7 on page 6 and also displayed below, appears on your display. Swiping upwards or pressing any key on the keyboard, displays a second screen (see Fig. 1.8 on page 7) in which you enter your user password after which Windows opens with a screen similar to that of Fig. 1.9 on page 7, also shown for my laptop in Fig. 2.2 on the next page.

12:00
Sunday 2 August

Fig. 2.1 A Windows 10 Start Screen.

Note: Most swipe movements of your finger on a touch sensitive screen correspond to dragging the mouse pointer on a PC. Similarly, tapping on such touch-screen devices corresponds to clicking the left mouse button. Touch and hold corresponds to a right-click of the mouse button.

Fig. 2.2 The Desktop with the Start Menu Activated.

The display shown in Fig. 2.2 is the two column **Start** screen, with the left column allowing access to **All Apps**, **Power options**, **Settings** and **File Explorer**, as well as most used Apps by simply tapping or clicking the listed entries, while the right column displays tiled icons that, when tapped or clicked, open the selected App. To see more such Apps, either swipe upwards or scroll down.

The actual **Desktop** shown in Fig. 2.3 is for my laptop and is the same as the **Desktop** I had before the Windows 10 upgrade. Yours might be different

Fig. 2.3 The Windows 10 Desktop on my Laptop.

To switch between the **Desktop** and an App screen, tap or  click the **Start** button at the bottom-left corner of the **Desktop** screen shown here (alternatively, press the **Windows ▪** key on the keyboard), then tap or click on the App of your choice. To return to the **Desktop** screen, close the App window by tapping or clicking on its **Close** button ☒ at the top right corner of the screen - it only lights up red when the mouse pointer is placed on it, otherwise it is grey, as are the other two buttons next to it – more about this later.

The Taskbar Area

Next to the **Start** button, is **Cortana**, the **Task View**, **Internet Explorer**, **File Explorer** and Windows **Store** buttons shown separately in Fig. 2.4 below.

Fig. 2.4.

To the right of the **Taskbar** you'll find the battery **Power and sleep settings** indicator (for a laptop or a tablet), the **Internet access** indicator, the **New Notifications** button and the **Touch keyboard**. To the right of this you'll find a Digital clock, as shown in Fig. 2.5 below, and to the extreme right of the **Taskbar** area, a thin strip which when tapped of clicked toggles between all open Apps and programs by minimising them and the **Desktop**.

14:06
05/08/2015   Fig. 2.5.

Tapping or clicking the Digital clock display, opens the screen in Fig. 2.6 and selecting the **Date and time settings** link at the bottom of the screen, displays the **Time & Language screen**, shown in Fig. 2.7 on the next page.

Fig. 2.6 The Change Date and Time Screen.

On this screen you find links to change the date and time formats, create additional date, time & regional settings and add clocks for different time zones. This can be very useful if you have friends living in different time zones and want to avoid waking them up!

Fig. 2.7 The Windows 10 Time & Language Settings Screen.

Here I show the display when I hover the mouse pointer over the **Date/Time** area after adding two more clocks to the local time.

Running Apps or Programs

With Windows 10, as indeed with Windows 8 & 8.1, you can choose programs and Apps to pin to the **Taskbar** and display as shown in Fig. 2.8.

Fig. 2.8.

To pin an App or program on the **Taskbar**, tap or click the

Fig. 2.9.

Start button, swipe upwards or scroll to find the tile representing the program or App you want to pin on the **Taskbar**, right-click it and select **Pin to taskbar**, as shown in Fig. 2.9.

Alternatively, touch and hold the selected tile, then tap the ⊙ icon that displays, tap the **More options** on the displayed list, then tap **Pin to taskbar**, as shown in Fig. 2.10.

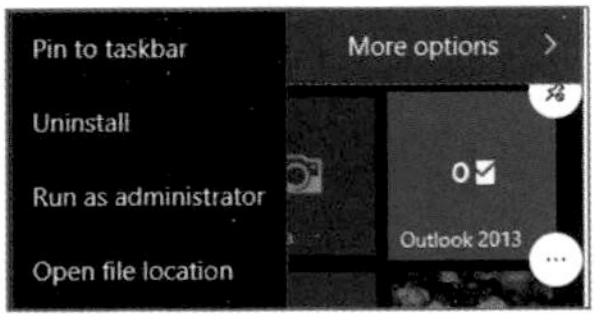

Note that in Fig. 2.8, three of the pinned programs on the **Taskbar** appear underlined which indicates that they are running. To verify this, tap or click the **Task View** button (the first in Fig. 2.8) to display Fig. 2.11 below.

Fig. 2.10.

Fig. 2.11 Thumbnails Showing Programs or Apps.

Tapping the '**X**' button at the top right corner of selected thumbnail, closes the running program or App. Moving the mouse pointer towards that area lights up the **Close**  button in red and clicking it closes the selected program or App.

You can also force a running App to close (stop running) by right-clicking on its thumbnail and selecting **Close** from the displayed menu

> **Note:** Apps or programs you have accessed during a session continue running until you close them.

Finally, you can access any of these running Apps or programs by tapping or clicking on its thumbnail.

Pinned programs on the **Taskbar** can be run by just tapping or clicking on their icon.

The System Tray

On the extreme right of the **Taskbar**, also called the **System Tray** (where the **Date/Time** area is), you'll find other icons, including the **Touch keyboard** and **Notifications** icons

Fig. 2.12 The System Tray.

which show the status of your system. To the right of the **Date/Time** area there is a very thin vertical strip which when tapped or clicked minimises all running Apps and programs and reveals the **Desktop**.

Tapping or clicking the up arrowhead to the left of the **System Tray**, reveals additional hidden (by default) icons, such as the **Speakers**, **Touch-Pad**, etc., as shown in Fig. 2.13. .

Other **System Tray** icons (in Fig. 2.12) show the **Power & sleep settings** of your computer 🔋 (for a laptop) and wireless connection 📶.

Fig. 2.13.

What is shown on the **System Tray** of your computer might be different, depending on your configuration.

When you point to some icons on the **System Tray**, an

Fig. 2.14.

information bubble opens showing the status for that setting as shown in Fig. 2.14. Other icons do not display such a bubble, in which case you'll have to tap or click them. For example, tapping or clicking the **Power & sleep settings** ⬚ icon, displays more detailed information, as shown in Fig. 2.15.

Fig. 2.15 Power Settings.

Try tapping or clicking the **Volume** icon ⬚ to open the volume controls so you can control the loudness of your PC or laptop speakers.

Creating Additional User Accounts

Windows allows a whole family to share a computer, with each person having their own set-up. Each account tells Windows what files and folders the holder can access, what changes can be made to the computer and controls their personal preferences. To add a new user, tap or click on the **Start** button and select **Settings** from the menu in Fig. 2.16.

Next, tap or click the **Accounts** option shown in Fig. 2.17 to display the screen in Fig. 2.18 on the next page.

Fig. 2.16 The Start Menu.

Fig. 2.17 The Settings Screen.

Fig. 2.18 The Accounts Screen.

As you can see, there are several options listed in Fig. 2.18 which can help you change your account settings or create additional accounts, etc., but first you must sign in. Next, tap or click **Family & other users** and in the next displayed screen, tap or click the **Add a family member** ➕ button. You are also given the option to 'Add someone else to the PC'.

If you choose to add a family member, you get to choose between an 'adult' or a 'child'. You are then asked to specify the person's e-mail address and if he or she hasn't got one, you are offered to create one @outlook.com. There are several more screens which ask you to supply appropriate information. Just follow the on screen instruction – it is that simple!

Personalising Your PC

You can personalise your PC's settings by tapping or clicking the **Personalisation** (awful word!) option shown in Fig. 2.17 on page 23, which displays the screen shown in Fig. 2.19.

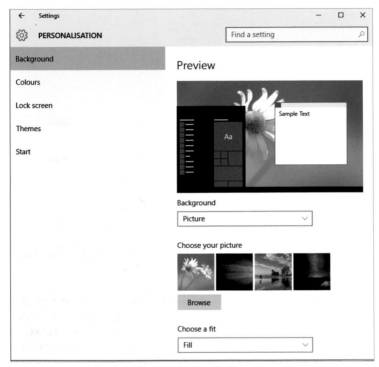

Fig. 2.19 Personalisation Settings Screen.

From this screen, you can change the desktop background of your PC, by either choosing one of the listed pictures, or select your own background by selecting the **Browse** button and navigating to where you keep your pictures.

Other options allow you to select **Colours**, to change the **Lock screen**, change **Themes** (to be discussed next) and control what Apps show and in what format on your **Start** menu. With most of the options, you are offered a **Preview** so you can see for yourself prior to committing to a change.

Windows Themes

Selecting **Themes** from the **Personalisation** screen, displays what is shown in Fig. 2.20 below.

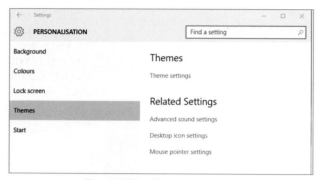

Fig. 2.20 The Themes Screen.

From here you can change the **Theme settings**, access the **Advanced sound settings**, change what icons appear on your desktop via the **Desktop icon settings** and change the appearance of your mouse via the **Mouse pointer settings**.

Windows comes with three default **Theme settings** which include most of the above changes at once, namely **Windows**, **Windows 10** and **Flowers**, as shown in Fig. 2.21. You can also get additional themes online.

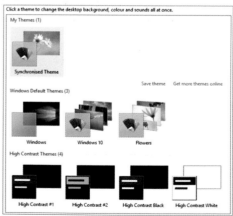

Fig. 2.21 The Theme Settings Screen.

Perhaps it might be worth having a look at the **Mouse pointer settings** (see Fig. 2.20) which, when tapped or clicked, displays the multi-tab screen shown in Fig. 2.22 on the next page with the **Pointer Options** tab selected.

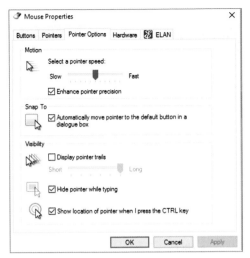

Fig. 2.22 The Mouse Properties Screen.

I suggest that you examine all the other **Related Settings**, but for the time being, at least, leave these as they are set at present. You can always come back later and change them, if you so wish.

Selecting a Screen Saver

In the previous Windows version, there was a **Screen Saver** link at the very bottom in the **Theme Settings** screen, but in Windows 10 it has been removed (see Fig. 2.21) and is difficult to find! So, if you would like to activate a screen saver on your laptop, go to the **Personalisation** screen in (Fig. 2.20) and type 'screen saver' in the search area at the top right of the screen. This opens the screen below.

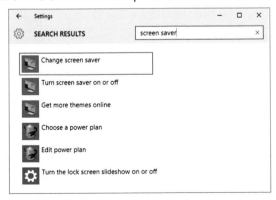

Fig. 2.23 The Results of Searching for Screen Saver.

Selecting the second search result (**Turn screen saver on or off**) displays the screen shown in Fig. 2.24 below in which I have already chosen the **Photos** folder as my preference under **Screen saver**.

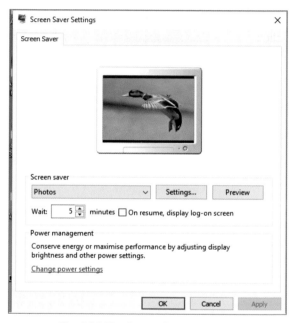

Fig. 2.24 The Screen Saver Settings.

You can change this selection by tapping or clicking the down-arrow on the **Screen saver** box to reveal a drop-down menu of the installed screen savers you can choose from, but it depends on personal preferences.

In this window you can also change the time of inactivity before the screen saver starts up. With some screen savers, clicking the **Settings** button displays a box for you to control their display settings. When you make all the changes you want, tap or click the **Preview** button to see the effect of the selected options in full screen. When you are happy, stop the preview, then tap or click the **Apply** button followed by the **OK** button.

Controlling Your System

The main way of controlling your PC or tablet, is through the **Control Panel** which provides quick and easy ways to change the hardware and software settings of your system. You can access the **Control Panel** by touching and holding or right-clicking the **Start** button menu (see Fig. 1.20, page 16) which opens the screen shown in Fig. 2.25 below.

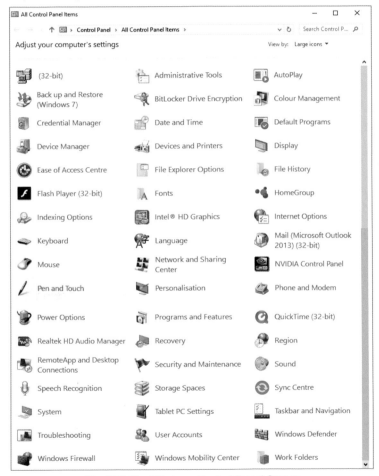

Fig. 2.25 The Windows Control Panel Screen.

From here you can add new hardware, remove or change programs, change the display type and its resolution, control your computer's setup and security, and a lot more besides. However daunting this may look, it is a very good idea to get familiar with the **Control Panel** features. Once you know your way around it, you can set up Windows just the way it suits you. The actual options available in **Control Panel** depend on your hardware and your version of Windows 10.

Changing the Windows Display

Display Windows requires the highest possible screen resolution that your graphics card is capable of delivering so that it can give you better text clarity, sharper images, and fit more items on your screen. At lower resolutions, less items fit on the screen, and images may have jagged edges. For example, a display resolution of 1024 x 768 pixels (picture elements) is low, while 1600 x 900 pixels or higher, is better.

Whether you can increase your screen resolution depends on the size and capability of your monitor and the type of video card installed in your PC. To find out if you can do this, use the **Display** icon in the **Control Panel** (Fig. 2.25 on previous page), to open the **Display** screen, then select the **Adjust resolution** link, to open the screen below.

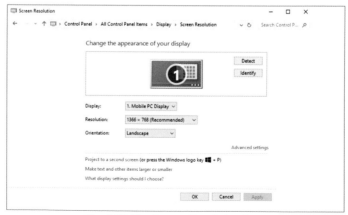

Fig. 2.26 The Screen Resolution Box.

Fig. 2.27 The Windows
Display Resolution.

Tapping or clicking the down arrow to the right of the **Resolution** box, opens a drop-down box similar to the one shown in Fig. 2.27, with your monitor's resolution settings and capabilities. It is best to select the highest possible resolution available.

From the display in Fig. 2.26, you can also arrange to **Project to a second screen**, if you have a larger monitor connected to your system.

Controlling Devices and Printers

When your computer was first set up, your devices and printers should have been installed automatically. If not, select the **Devices and Printers** icon (shown above) from the **Control Panel** to open the screen shown in Fig. 2.28 below.

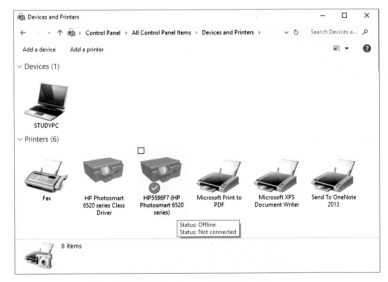

Fig. 2.28 The Devices and Printers Screen.

My **Devices and Printers** screen displays one device and six printers, one of which is a Fax. In the case of the printers, one is an air printer (the default), one for creating formatted print (Microsoft XPS) documents and three more printers, one of which is a network printer.

With Windows 10, most devices and printers are automatically detected at upgrade time, or during the boot-up process. So if you add a new printer or a new device, like a camera, to your system it should be recognised. You may be asked for the necessary driver files if they are not already in the Windows directory, but these should come on a CD, or can be found on the manufacturer's Web site.

Configuring Your Printer

To control your printer, double-tap or double-click its icon in the **Devices and Printers** screen (Fig. 2.28), to open a 'Printer Control' window like that shown in Fig. 2.29 below.

Fig. 2.29 The Printer Control Window.

From here you can control what is waiting to be printed, set preferences and customise your printer. Other device options specific to the printer might also display. In your case these will most certainly be different.

A newly installed printer is automatically set as the default printer, indicated by a green ✅ tick against it in the **Devices and Printers** screen. To change the default printer, double tap or double-click the required printer.

Once you have installed and configured your printers, the quickest way to print a simple document or file is to print using Windows itself. Locate the file that you want to print in a folder, maybe **Documents**, touch and hold or right-click it, and select **Print** from the displayed menu. Windows will print it using your default printer settings.

Managing Print Jobs

If you want to find out what is happening when you have sent documents to your printer, double-tap or double-click the printer icon 🖨 in the **System Tray** on the right of the **Taskbar**, to open the **Print Queue**.

Fig. 2.30 The Print Queue.

This displays detailed information about the work actually being printed, or of print jobs that are waiting in the queue. This includes the name of the document, its status and 'owner', when it was added to the print queue, the printing progress and when printing was started.

You can control the printing operations from the **Printer** and **Document** menu options of the **Print Queue** window. Selecting **Printer**, **Pause Printing** will stop the operation until you make the same selection again. The **Cancel All Documents** option will remove all the print jobs from the queue, but it sometimes takes a while.

> **Note:** If an error occurs with a print job, it will be necessary to use the **Cancel All Documents** option, before you can print anything else.

Working with Programs

Installing programs on your computer is very easy with Windows 10. Just place the CD or DVD that the software came on in the appropriate drive and Windows will start the installation process automatically. If you downloaded the program from the Internet, it should run and install itself. Use the **Programs and Features** icon on the **Control Panel** (shown above) or tap and hold or right-click the **Start** button to open the screen shown in Fig. 2.31. Your contents will be different, obviously!

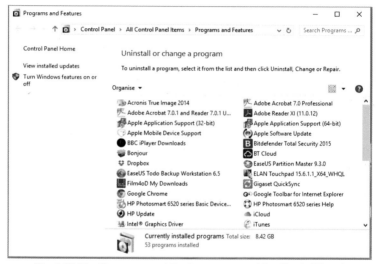

Fig. 2.31 The Programs and Features screen of the Control Panel.

Uninstalling or Changing a Program

Changing an already installed program or uninstalling one is very easy with Windows. To do either, select the program you want to work with. After selecting a program, three extra options may appear to the right of **Organize**; namely, **Uninstall**, **Change** and **Repair**. However, with some programs **Change** and/or **Repair** are not available, while with others **Change** is replaced by the **Repair** option only. Try it!

Using the option to **Uninstall** a program, removes all trace of it from your hard disc, although sometimes the folders are left empty on your hard drive.

> **Note:** Be careful with this application, because selecting a program on the list might remove it without further warning!

Running a Program as Administrator

If a program that you are trying to run gives you errors such as **Access Denied** or **No Permission**, then running it as an administrator can usually give the permission it needs to run properly. With Windows, an administrator is someone allowed to make changes on a computer that will affect other users. These include security settings, installing software and hardware, and being able to access all files on the computer.

Somewhat confusingly even if your account is set up as an **Administrator** you will still be prompted to give 'Administrator' rights at certain times. There is a 'Hidden Administrator' account with full powers over your computer and this is the one you sometimes have to access.

> **Note:** You should only allow a program that you trust to run as administrator as once you have given full permission, it will have complete access to your computer.

If you are doing this while logged in as a standard user instead of an administrator, then you will need to provide the administrator's password before the program will run as administrator.

3

The File Explorer & OneDrive

You use the **File Explorer** (shown on the left) to explore the

 files on your PC, while you use the **OneDrive** (formally known as **SkyDrive**), shown on the right, to

save your work on a drive in the Cloud.

The File Explorer and its Folders

In both Windows 10 and its predecessors every user starts with their own Apps, programs and a set of data folders called simply **Desktop**, **Downloads**, **Documents**, **Pictures** and any **Cloud** folders you might have. To see these, tap or click the **File Explorer** button ![button] on the **Taskbar** to open a window similar to that in Fig. 3.1.

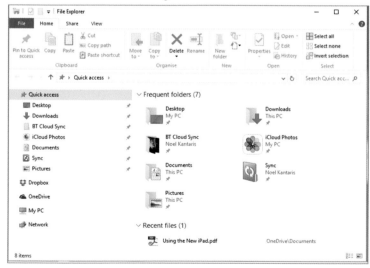

Fig. 3.1 A Set of Personal Folders.

Libraries first introduced in Windows 7, are turned off in Windows 10 by default. Although you can switch them on, if you so wish, but it involves tinkering with the **Registry** which is best left alone, unless you are a real expert – it is very easy to mess up the **Registry** and make your computer unusable!

The left pane of the **File Explorer** window, called the **Navigation** pane, lists a tree-style view of your personal folders, while the right pane lists the folders and files in the selected personal folder in the **Navigation** pane. Tapping or clicking such a folder in the **Navigation** pane opens its contents in the right pane.

Folders are just containers in which you can store files or other folders. Arranging files into logical groups in folders makes it easier to locate and work with them. For example in Fig. 3.2 below, folders (and if you scroll further down) files within the **Documents** folder are displayed on the right pane.

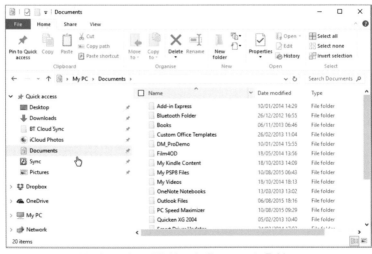

Fig. 3.2 A Set of Folders in Documents Folder.

Double-tapping or double-clicking a folder (Books in this case) opens it and displays its contents as shown in Fig. 3.3 on the next page.

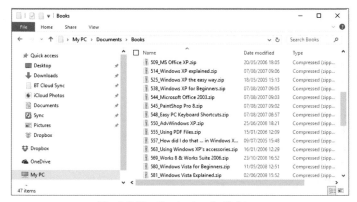

Fig. 3.3 The Contents of a Folder.

Files contain related information, such as a word-processed letter, a digital photo, a spreadsheet, a video or a music track.

Parts of a File Explorer Window

In Fig. 3.4, a typical Windows 10 **File Explorer** window is shown with its constituent parts labelled and later described.

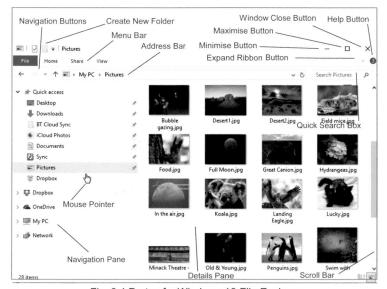

Fig. 3.4 Parts of a Windows 10 File Explorer.

You may have noticed by now that the buttons on the toolbars of the different **File Explorer** windows change to reflect the type of work you can do in that type of window. For example, tapping or clicking a picture, displays the **Picture Tools** label above the **Menu bar** and also displays a **Ribbon** with appropriate tools to **Edit** or **View** pictures, as shown in Fig. 3.5. The **Ribbon** will be discussed shortly.

Fig. 3.5 The Picture Tools Ribbon.

Once you open one **Ribbon** or used the **Expand Ribbon** ⌄ button (see Fig. 3.4 for its location), then tapping or clicking each **Menu** bar option (apart from **File**), displays different but appropriate ribbons allowing you to work with the selected option. You can close the **Ribbon** by tapping or clicking the **Minimise Ribbon** ⌃ button which replaces the **Expand Ribbon** ⌄ button, once the ribbon has been expanded.

The typical **File Explorer** window is subdivided into several areas which have the following functions:

Area	Function
Minimise button –	Tapping or clicking the **Minimise** button stores a window and its contents as an icon on the **Taskbar**. Clicking on such an icon will restore the window
Maximise button ▫	Tapping or clicking the **Maximise** button fills the screen with the active window. When that happens, the **Maximise** button changes to a **Restore Down** button ▫ which can be used to restore the window to its former size.
Close button ✕	The extreme top right button that you tap or click to close a window.

Navigation buttons	The **Go Back** (left) button takes you to the previous display, while the **Go Forward** (right) button takes you to the next display. The down-arrow ▼ gives access to **Recent Locations**.
↑	Tapping or clicking this button takes you one level up towards the **Desktop**.
Address bar 	Shows the location of the current folder. You can change locations here, or switch to an **Internet Explorer** window by typing a Web address.
Quick search box	The box in which you type your search criteria. As you start typing, the displayed files filter down to just the matching terms, making it much easier to find your files.
Menu bar	The bar allows you to choose from several menu options. Tapping or clicking on a menu item displays the pull-down menu associated with it.
Toolbar	A bar of icons that you tap or click to carry out some common actions (see Fig. 3.5). The icons displayed depend on the type of window.
Scroll bars/buttons	The bars/buttons at the extreme right and bottom of each window (or pane within a window) that contain a scroll box/button. Tapping or clicking on these, allows you to see parts of a document that might not be visible in that size window.
Mouse pointers	The arrow which appears when the pointer is placed over menus, scroll bars, buttons and lists or the hand that displays when pointing to a link.

The File Menu Bar Option

Tapping or clicking the **File** option on a window's menu bar, displays a screen similar to the one shown in Fig. 3.6. In this case the **Help** option was selected to show you where to find it. Each listed option under **File** displays different options in the **Details** pane.

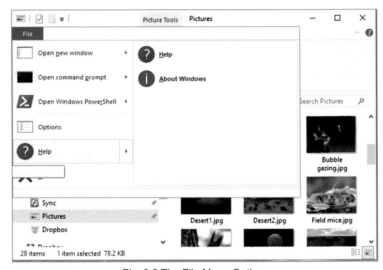

Fig. 3.6 The File Menu Option.

Items on the sub-menu marked with an arrow to their right ▶, open up additional options when selected.

> **Note:** Having activated the **File** menu, you can close it without taking any further action by simply tapping or clicking outside its window, or by pressing the **Esc** key on the keyboard. If you select the **Close** option instead, you will exit the **File Explorer** altogether.

Manipulating Windows

To use any Windows program effectively, including the **File Explorer**, you need to be able to move a window or re-size it so that you can see all of it.

Changing the active window – If you have several windows open on the screen, you can make one active by simply tapping or clicking it or, if it is not visible, tap or click its icon on the **Taskbar**. In the case of running Apps, tap or click the **Task View** button (the first after the **Cortana** bar on the **Taskbar** to open the thumbnails of the Apps display (see Fig. 2.11 on page 21), then tap or click on the one you want.

Moving a window – To move a window, point to its **Title** bar with either your finger or the mouse, tap it or click it and then drag it until it is where you want it on the screen. You can only do this if the window does not occupy the full screen and it has a maximise button □ visible.

Minimising and maximising windows – To minimise a window into a **Taskbar** icon, tap or click the **Minimise** button ‾ in the upper-right corner of the window. To maximise a window so that it fills the entire screen, tap or click the **Maximise** button □ , or double-tap or double-click in the **Title** bar. Double-tapping/clicking again will restore it.

A window that has been minimised or maximised can be returned to its original size and position on the screen by either tapping or clicking on its **Taskbar** icon to expand it to a window, or tapping or clicking on the **Restore Down** button ⟲ of a maximised window, to reduce it to its former size.

 Re-sizing a window – To change the size of a window either place your finger on a visible edge of the window, or corner, and drag the edge or corner to the required place. With the mouse, the pointer first changes to a two-headed arrow when placed at the edge or corner, as shown here, before you can drag.

Closing a window – To close a window and save screen space and memory, tap or click the **Close** ▬ button.

Additional Sizing Features

Windows 10 also includes some additional ways to manipulate windows, whether those of a program or an App.

Maximising windows – To maximise the active window, first tap or click its **Title** bar (the top bar of each window that includes the name of the App), then drag it up towards the top of the screen. When the top edge of the window touches the top of the screen, the window will maximise.

Snapping windows to the edge of the screen – This allows the display of two (or four) windows side by side, each taking half the width of your screen (or if displaying four, a quarter of the screen). In Fig. 3.7, two windows are shown side-by-side.

Fig. 3.7 Two Windows Displaying Side-by-side.

To achieve this, drag one window to the left by its **Title** bar. When the edge of the window hits the left side of the screen, the window will snap to that edge and re-size to occupy the left half of the screen. Next, drag a second window towards the right screen edge to re-size it and snap it to the right half of the screen.

Snapping windows to the four corners of the screen – To see a four window arrangement on a screen, each occupying one quarter of the screen, have a look at Fig. 1.16 on page 14. The windows of the displayed running Apps are snapped to the four corners of the screen by dragging them in succession towards each corner.

Restoring a maximised or snapped window – Drag the window by its **Title** bar towards the centre of the screen.

The Ribbon

The **Ribbon** is a device that presents commands organised into a set of tabs, as shown in Fig.3.8. It replaces traditional menus and toolbars found in non-Microsoft Apps or programs.

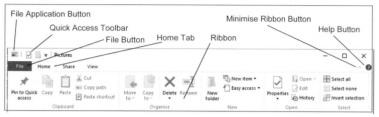

Fig. 3.8 The Home Tab of the Pictures Ribbon.

The tabs on the **Ribbon** display the commands that are most relevant for each of the task areas in an App or program activity (in this case), as shown above for the **Pictures** App.

Note the **Minimise the Ribbon** ⌃ button which you tap or click to gain more space on your screen. It then changes to the **Expand the Ribbon** ⌄ button, which you tap or click to display the **Ribbon** again.

Also note that there are three basic components to the Ribbon, as shown in Fig. 3.9 below.

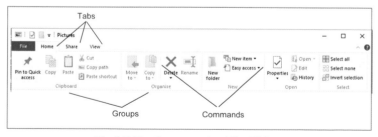

Fig. 3.9 The Components of the Ribbon.

The Ribbon Components are:

Tabs   There are several basic tabs across the top, each representing an activity area.

Groups   Each tab has several groups that show related items together.

Commands   A command can be a button or a box to read or enter information.

For each activity the **Home** tab contains all the things you use most often, such as creating a **New** folder, the **Copy** and **Delete** commands, etc. Tapping or clicking a new tab opens a new series of groups, each with its relevant command buttons. This really works very well.

Contextual tabs also appear, as we have seen earlier, when they are needed so that you can very easily find and use the commands needed for the current operation.

Below the content of the other three **Ribbon** tabs is displayed.

Fig. 3.10 The Share Tab of the Pictures Ribbon.

Fig. 3.11 The View Tab of the Pictures Ribbon.

Fig. 3.12 The Manage Tab of the Pictures Ribbon.

The OneDrive

Microsoft's **OneDrive** is one of the best Web storage services available. You get 30 GB free Web space to store you photos (15 GB) and documents (another 15 GB) so you can access them from wherever you happen to be. You can also invite your friends to join **OneDrive** in which case, you and your friend get an additional 0.5 GB each (up to a total of 5 GB). You can also invite other users to access your files for sharing or editing shared documents.

OneDrive is pre-installed on Windows 10 and is found on the **Navigation** pane of the **File Explorer**, as shown here. If you have already used **SkyDrive** (the predecessor to **OneDrive**), tapping or clicking this item, displays your **Documents** and **Pictures** folders held on **OneDrive**, otherwise it opens a screen similar to that in Fig. 3.13.

Fig. 3.13 The Initial OneDrive Screen.

Tapping or clicking the **Get started** button, displays a screen for you to sign in, using your Microsoft account's details, namely your e-mail address. This is necessary for security purposes. Having done so, you can now view your folders and files on **OneDrive**.

Creating a Folder on OneDrive

You can create additional folders or sub-folders on **OneDrive** by selecting **OneDrive** on the **Navigation**, pane of the **File Explorer**, then tapping or clicking the **New Folder** command button on the **Ribbon**. This creates a new folder which then awaits for a name of your choice to be typed in to replace the default name **'New Folder'**, as shown in Fig. 3.14 below. Call this new folder **Pictures**.

Fig. 3.14 The Contents of my OneDrive with Toolbar Active.

Once this is done, the easiest way to copy files to **OneDrive** is to open the newly created folder, then navigate to **My PC** and tap or click the **Pictures** folder to open it. Next, select the pictures you want to send to **OneDrive** and drag them (by holding the **Ctrl** and **Shift** keys down while doing so) to copy them to the **Pictures** folder on **OneDrive**. This process is shown in Fig. 3.15 on the next page.

If you don't hold the **Ctrl** key down while you are dragging such files to a new location, you will be moving them out of their present location rather than copying them and retaining a copy on your PC.

It is important to open the folder into which you want to copy the folder/files and be precise in your dragging technique, otherwise they might be copied to a different folder!

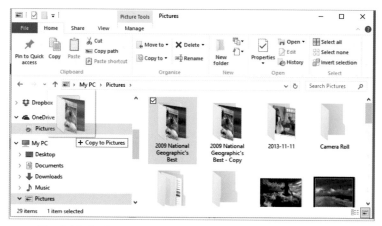

Fig. 3.15 The Process of Copying a Pictures Folder to OneDrive.

If you find this method too difficult, don't worry, as an alternative method of doing the same thing will be discussed in the next section of this chapter.

You should only save files in your **OneDrive**, either as an additional backup or because you might want to access them when away from home. The idea behind this is that you use **OneDrive** as the place in which to hold your documents, photos, etc., and allow your PC, tablet and phone running Windows 10 to synchronise with **OneDrive**.

What this means is that you can access your documents no matter where you are, on any of your devices. Any changes you make to a file on any of your devices is applied to your **OneDrive** file. However, to view and change your **OneDrive** files, you must be connected to the Internet.

An additional benefit of **OneDrive** is that you can create a specific folder on it that its contents can be 'shared' by specified friends or colleagues to whom you have given access rights to, so that they can easily view and interact or collaborate with your work.

Zipping Files

You can use the **File Explorer** to zip files prior to uploading them to **OneDrive**. This will help to keep you within your allocated free space on **OneDrive**, as **Zipped** files are a lot smaller than the originals from which they were created. You do this as follows:

- Start **File Explorer** and go to a place on your hard disc were you can select a large file to upload, as shown in the example in Fig. 3.16.

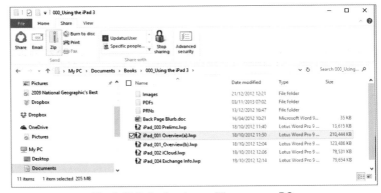

Fig. 3.16 Selecting Large Files on your PC.

- In the **Share** tab, activate the **Zip** option.

- The selected file (which is more that 210 MB in size) will be zipped in a folder using the same name.

In Fig. 3.18, shown on the next page, you can see a drag and drop operation using the **File Explorer**. However, to be able to carry out this operation, you'll need to open two **File Explorer** windows as discussed next.

First, start **File Explorer** and locate **OneDrive** on your **Folder List**, then create a new folder in **OneDrive** and call it **Documents**. Finally, open this folder on your **OneDrive** and size the **Documents** window to something similar to that on the right of Fig. 3.18 on the next page.

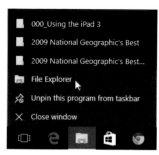

Fig. 3.17 The Right-click File
Explorer Menu.

Next, touch and hold or right-click the **File Explorer** icon on the **Task** bar and select the **File Explorer**, pointed to on the displayed menu in Fig. 3.17. Only the lower half of the menu is shown in Fig. 3.17.

This is the only way to open two **File Explorer** windows on the screen at the same time.

Next, size and move the newly opened window next to the **OneDrive**, **Documents** window and locate the file you want to upload on your hard disc. In this case, the 100 MB original file is zipped and compressed to less than half of its original size. Finally, drag the zipped file from the left window and drop it in the **Documents** window, as shown in Fig. 3.18.

Fig. 3.18 Dragging and Dropping a Zipped File into the Documents Folder of OneDrive.

You could, of course, use the easier way described in Fig. 3.15 on page 49.

Finally, revert to the **File Explorer** to see the zipped file in your **OneDrive**, **Documents** folder. Tapping or clicking such a file opens it in **OneDrive** from where you can retrieve the original file provided your PC has the program that created the original file installed, as shown in Fig. 3.19 on the next page.

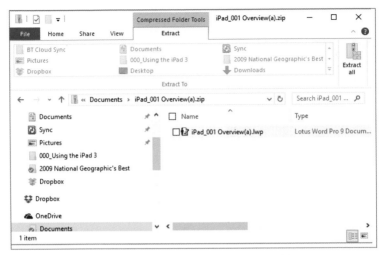

Fig. 3.19 Selecting Large Files on your PC.

Uploading a PDF File

If you have a very large file and you want to be able to refer to it on a mobile device, but you haven't got to edit it, then perhaps the best solution is to convert the file to PDF format and upload that version.

For example, part of a book with a total word processed file size of 730 MB, can be reduced to just under 4 MB when converted to PDF format. That size file can then be uploaded using the drag and drop desktop method described on previous pages of this chapter. Taping or clicking such a file opens it for you to examine on a mobile device.

4

Edge & Internet Explorer

Microsoft Edge is the new Internet browser in Windows 10, shown on the left (although **Internet Explorer**, is still there in the tiled Apps column of the **Start** menu, shown on the right). The latter is retained as it supports specific legacy Apps and plug-ins that are not supported by the new browser. So, we shall examine both of these Web browser Apps/programs.

The Microsoft Edge Browser

When you first open **Microsoft Edge**, by tapping or clicking either its **Taskbar** shortcut or its tile on the **Start** menu, a screen similar to that in Fig. 4.1 is displayed.

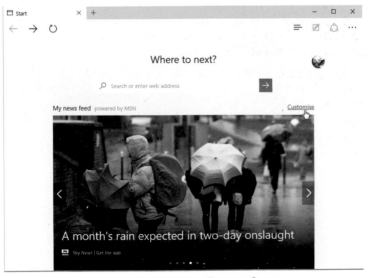

Fig. 4.1 A Microsoft Edge Browser Screen.

Gone is the uncluttered screen of **Internet Explorer**! Now you get instant information about your local weather and news, but before you can watch their video you'll have to put up with annoying adverts.

Luckily, **Microsoft Edge** can be customised by tapping or clicking the **Customise** link pointed to in Fig. 4.1. Tapping or clicking that link, opens a **Customise** window, as shown in Fig. 4.2 below.

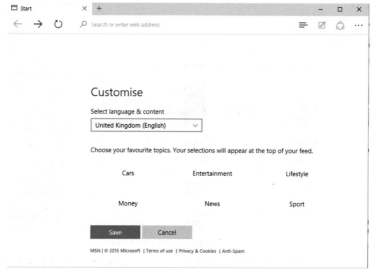

Fig. 4.2 The Customise Screen for Microsoft Edge.

Chose your favourite topics and tap or click the **Save** button. I chose News only, but it did not eliminate the annoying adds!

Next, type in the **Search** box in Fig. 4.1 a search criteria, such as shown below in Fig. 4.3

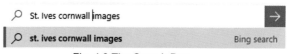

Fig. 4.3 The Search Box.

As you type, **bing** (the default search engine) offers suggestions which you might like to accept.

If you want the result of your search to be confined to a county or the UK only, then you must include the county name and/or the country. On tapping or clicking the blue arrow, the search is completed and a screen similar to that in Fig. 4.4 appears.

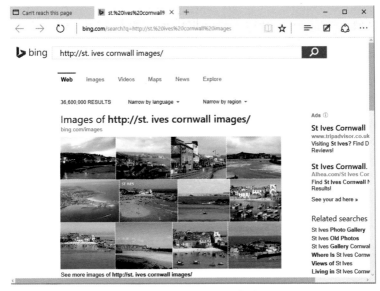

Fig. 4.4 The Result of a Specific Search.

Note what **bing** has inserted into the **Address** bar at the top of the screen, and reproduced below.

http://st.ives cornwall images/

This is known as the URL which stands for Uniform Resource Locator of the Web page and it appears in the **Address** bar. Before you search for something else, have a look at the very top of the **bing** screen, shown enlarged in Fig. 4.5.

Fig. 4.5 The Bing Search Topics.

As you can see above, you can direct your search to specifics, such as the Web (the default), **Images**, **Videos**, **Maps**, etc. So, to search for images, first select **Images**.

You can also search the **Videos** option, where you'll find some very interesting videos of St. Ives – you could almost have your holiday here and now without the bother of travel!

To exit a Website, either type a new URL of a Web page in the **Address** bar, or tap/click the **Close** ☒ button (top-right corner in Fig. 4.4 shown on the previous page). The **Close** button only turns red when you point to it with the mouse.

The Address Bar

There are many millions of Web pages to look at on the Web, so where do you start? In **Microsoft Edge** the **Address** bar is where you type or paste, the address or URL of a Web page you want to open.

For example, typing what is displayed in the **Address** bar below, shown in Fig. 4.6, then tapping or clicking the **Go** → button will open the list of books page on my personal Web site. In this way (knowing the full URL), selecting the **Go** button, goes directly to the page stated, without activating the **bing** search engine.

Fig. 4.6 The Address Bar.

The **Address** bar is the main way of opening new Web pages when you know their URLs. A drop-down menu of the most recent locations you have entered, will be offered by **Microsoft Edge**.

Web Browser Buttons

Microsoft Edge is fully equipped with toolbars, which have buttons you can tap or click to quickly carry out various actions, as show in Fig. 4.7.

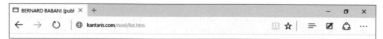

Fig. 4.7 The Web Browser Buttons.

The **Microsoft Edge** buttons have the following functionality:

Button	Function
← **Back**	Displays the previous page viewed. If there isn't one this is 'greyed out'.
→ **Forward**	Displays the next page on the **History** list.
↻ **Refresh**	Brings a fresh copy of the current Web page to the viewer.
☆ **Favourites**	Add to Favourites or Reading List.
≡ **Hub**	It includes Favourites, Reading List, History and Downloads.
☑ **Web Note**	Allows you to make a Web note. It displays a separate page with tools to be used, such as Pen, Highlighter, Eraser, ability to Type a note and ability to Clip a Web page.
♻ **Share**	It includes Favourites, Reading List, History and Downloads.
⋯ **More actions**	It includes open a New window, open an InPrivate window, Zoom, Find on page, Print, Pin to Start, ability to Open with Internet Explorer and Settings.

Microsoft Edge allows you to write comments on touch sensitive screens, use a highlighter or the keyboard to type your thoughts and read these later (see Fig. 1.24 on page 13). You can also choose to **Clip** a Web page, **Collapse** a typed message and/or save it. Tapping or clicking the **Exit** option at the top-right of the screen, removes all comments and returns the Web page in its original display.

You can use **Cortana** with **Microsoft Edge** which is worth exploring. If you say something that **Cortana** doesn't understand, instead of saying so, she says 'I cannot connect to the Internet right now, please try later'. Don't believe a word of it, just rephrase your request and speak more clearly!

Perhaps **Microsoft Edge** is more suited to tablets than a laptop or desktop. Personally, I prefer **Internet Explorer**'s uncluttered screen without any intruding adverts.

The Internet Explorer

To start the **Internet Explorer**, tap or click its icon on the **Start** screen. If you haven't used **Internet Explorer** before, a simple, uncluttered screen is displayed, as shown in Fig. 4.8 below.

Fig. 4.8 The Basic Internet Explorer Screen.

Desktop Internet Explorer Toolbars

Next, let us add a few toolbars on the screen so that **Internet Explorer** becomes easier to use. To do this, tap or click an empty part of the screen to the right of the **Address** bar to open the drop-down menu shown in Fig. 4.9 in which I have already made a selection of toolbars.

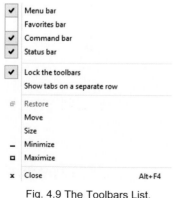

You can choose which toolbars to display by tapping or clicking the ones you want to see. This places a tick mark against the selected toolbar. Tapping or clicking again a selected toolbar, deselects it.

Fig. 4.9 The Toolbars List.

Fig. 4.10 shows what you'll see if all the toolbars on the list were to be selected as shown in Fig. 4.9.

Fig. 4.10 Internet Explorer with Toolbars.

Internet Explorer, like all other browser programs, requires a 'search engine' to work with it, being **Microsoft bing**, **Google** or some other search engine.

To select which search engine should be attached to the opening **Internet Explorer** screen, tap or click the **Tools** ⚙ button, pointed to in Fig. 4.11 below, to open the displayed menu options.

Next, select the **Internet options** entry to open the multi-tab screen shown in Fig. 4.12 on the next page.

Fig. 4.11 The Explorer Tools Menu Options.

Fig. 4.12 The Internet Options.

Next, replace the highlighted **About:blank** entry with **http://www.bing.com**, then tap or click the **Apply**, followed by the **OK** button

From now on, starting **Internet Explorer**, displays the **bing Home page** shown below in Fig. 4.13. If you want to replace the opening screen of **Internet Explorer**, you'll have to return to the **General** tab screen of Fig. 4.12 and change the URL in the **Home page** section.

The Bing Search Engine

The opening picture displayed in the **bing Home page**, changes daily, so what you see on your screen is bound to be different to the one below.

Fig. 4.13 The Bing Opening Screen.

Points of Interest

At the bottom of the **bing** screen, there is further information on the displayed picture, where it was taken and what is popular now in the news, as shown in Fig. 4.14, but that information also changes daily with the picture.

Fig. 4.14 Further Points of Interest.

The first button (top-right on the above screen dump) can be used to display the picture in 4.13 in full screen. However, while in full screen you can not see the information at the bottom of the screen as shown in Fig. 4.14 above.

The next two buttons can be used to go back to the previous day's picture or forward to the current day's picture, while the last button gives you information on the current screen.

> **Note:** There is a lot on this **bing** screen which you should open on your own display as it is impossible to enlarge it any further on the screen dump on Fig. 4.13.

The Bing Search Preferences

On the top-right of **bing**'s screen (see Fig. 4.13 on previous page), you'll find the **Preferences** 🔅 button. Tapping or clicking it, displays a menu allowing you to either **Search history** or access the **bing Settings** screen. In Fig. 4.15, shown on the next page, both the **Preferences** menu and the **Settings** screen are shown opened.

> **Note:** What is shown in Fig. 4.15 on the next page, is for the GENERAL preferences on **bing** with other screens available for WEB, HOMEPAGE, NEWS, etc. Do look at all of these and make any changes you need to, before tapping or clicking the Save button (you have to scroll down to see it) to make the changes permanent.

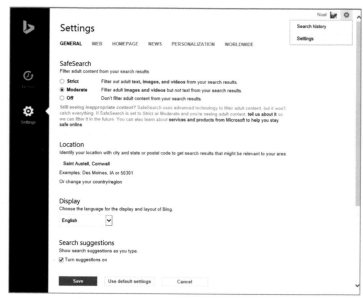

Fig. 4.15 The General Preferences Settings Screen.

Searching the Web

The top section of the **bing** screen, displayed in Fig. 4.13 on page 60, is shown enlarged in Fig. 4.16 below.

Fig. 4.16 The Bing Search Options and Search Box.

Note that you can specify what kind of results your search should return, whether WEB pages, IMAGES, VIDEOS, MAPS, etc., depending on the choice you've made at the very top of the screen. Your selected topic is displayed in orange.

To search for any type of images, first select IMAGES, then on the screen of endless displayed landscapes, type in the **Search** box the name of the town you want to see.

The search result for Falmouth is shown in Fig. 4.17 below.

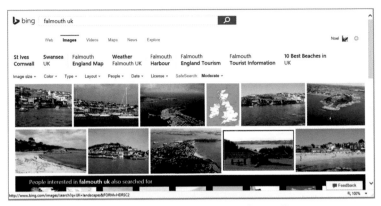

Fig. 4.17 Images of Falmouth in Cornwall.

You can also search the VIDEOS or MAPS option, where you could find interesting videos or maps of the area.

If you start another App, because you wanted to, say, check your mail, then selecting the **Internet Explorer** tile again, will returned you to the exact screen you were looking at before you left it. You will be forgiven if you thought that there is no way out of this Web page!

To exit a Web site, either type a new URL of a Web page in the **Address** bar or tap/click the **Close** ■ button (top-right corner in Fig. 4.13 on page 60 which only turns red when you point to it with the mouse). This last move also exits the **Internet Explorer** altogether. Next time you open **Internet Explorer**, it will display the current (that day's choice) **bing** Web picture.

Internet Explorer Buttons

As we have seen earlier, **Internet Explorer** is fully equipped with toolbars, which have buttons you can tap or click to quickly carry out various functions. To examine some of the buttons, the ones not yet discussed, open a Web page, such as the one shown in Fig. 4.18 on the next page.

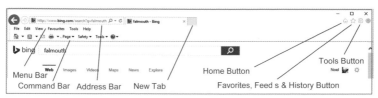

Fig. 4.18 The Internet Explorer Address Bar and Buttons.

Most of the buttons on the **Address** bar of the **Internet Explorer** (top of the screen - not **bing**'s) and other toolbars are pretty self-explanatory. Those on the **Explorer**'s **Address** bar have the following functions:

Button		Function
⬅	Back	Displays the previous page viewed. If there isn't one this is 'greyed out'.
➡	Forward	Displays the next page on the **History** list. If there isn't one this is 'greyed out'.
🔍	Search	Searches for the text typed into the **Explorer**'s **Search** box.
↻	Refresh	Brings a fresh copy of the current Web page to the viewer.
✕	Stop	Halts any on-line transfer of data.

Tapping or clicking the down-arrowhead at the extreme right of the **Status** bar (at the bottom of Fig. 4.17 on the previous page), opens a menu of **Zoom** options, as shown here in Fig. 4.19.

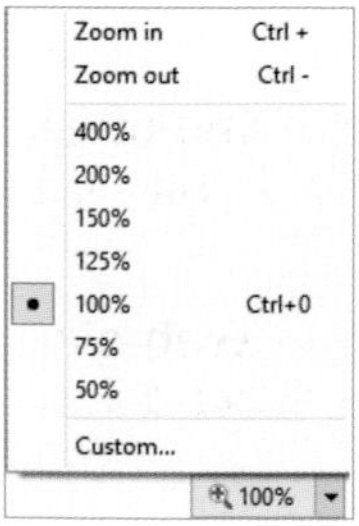

Zoom in	Ctrl +
Zoom out	Ctrl -
400%	
200%	
150%	
125%	
• 100%	Ctrl+0
75%	
50%	
Custom...	
🔍 100% ▼	

Fig. 4.19 Zoom Options.

The Menu Bar

The **Menu** bar is located below the **Explorer**'s **Address** bar (see Fig. 4.18 on previous page). It displays sub-menus when one of its menu options (**File**, **Edit**, **View**, **Favourites**, **Tools** or **Help** ❷) is selected. Fig. 4.20 shows the sub-menu of **Help** and what displays if you select the **About Internet Explorer** option.

Fig. 4.20 The Internet Options Dialogue Box.

Most of the **Menu** bar options are fairly self-explanatory, so I leave you to investigate them by yourself. The only option that merits deliberation in some detail is **Favourites**, to be discussed shortly.

The Command Bar

The **Command** bar, below the **Menu** toolbar (see Fig. 4.20 above), has the following default buttons:

Button	*Function*
🏠 **Home**	Displays your specified home page, with a Microsoft page as the default.
📡 **Feeds**	View Feeds on the open Web site. If a feed is not detected the colour of the icon remains grey.
✉ **Read Mail**	Opens your mail client so that you can read your e-mail messages.

	Print	Prints the open Web page, or frame, using the current print settings.
Page ▼		Opens a menu that allows you to open a new window, save the current page, send it or a link to send it by e-mail to a recipient, zoom the page, or change the text size on it.
Safety ▼		Displays a drop-down menu that allows you to delete the browsing **History**, browse in private, see the privacy policy of Web pages, turn on the **SmartScreen Filter** so that unsafe Web sites can be reported, and activate **Windows Update**.
Tools ▼		Displays a drop-down menu that allows you to diagnose connection problems, reopen the last browsing session, manage pop-ups, specify your Internet options, and generally control how **Explorer** works.
❓▼		Opens a drop-down menu giving quick access to **Help** topics.

The Favourites Bar

To add a **Favourites** bar, follow the instructions on page 58. Once activated, it includes the following buttons:

Button		*Function*
⭐	**Favourites**	Opens the **Favourites Center** from which you can choose the **Favourites**, **Feeds** or **History** bars.
⭐	**Add to**	Adds a favourite site to the **Favourites** bar.

In addition, there are links to suggested Microsoft Web sites.

Managing Favourites

Using **Favourites** (Bookmarks), is an easy way to save Web page addresses for future use. It's much easier to select a

page from a sorted list, than to manually type a URL address into the **Address** bar. You don't have to remember the address and are less likely to make a typing error!

With **Internet Explorer** your **Favourites** are kept in the **Favourites Center**, shown in Fig. 4.21, opened by tapping or clicking the **Open Favourites Center** button.

Fig. 4.21 Favourites Centre.

To keep the list open in a separate pane, tap/click the **Pin the Favourites Center** button. To unpin it, tap/click its **Close** button.

Adding a Favourite – There are several ways to add a **Favourite** to your list:

One way is to tap or click the **Add to Favourites** button to add the address of the Web page you are viewing to a **Favourites** bar which displays to the right of the **Add to Favourites** button. Another way is to touch and hold or right-click the Web page you are viewing and select **Add to Favourites** from the drop-down menu. This opens the **Add a Favourite** dialogue box (Fig. 4.22) in which you can give the new **Favourite** a name, and choose a folder to put it in. Then just tap or click the **Add** button to finish.

Fig. 4.22 The Add a Favourite Box.

Browsing History

Internet Explorer stores details of all the Web pages and files you view on your hard disc, and places temporary

pointers to them in a folder. To return to these in the future, tap or click the **History** tab in the **Favourites Centre**, to open the **History** list shown in Fig. 4.23.

In this list you can see what Web sites you visited in the last 3 weeks. Tapping or clicking a listed site opens links to the individual Web pages you went to. Selecting any of these will open the page again.

Fig. 4.23 Web Browsing History.

The length of time history items are kept on your hard disc can be set by using the **Tools** button and selecting **Internet Options** to open the tabbed dialogue box shown in Fig. 4.24.

Tapping or clicking the **Settings** button in the **Browsing history** section, pointed to here, opens an additional dialogue box in which you can select the number of days that **History** files are kept (between 0 and 999) in the **History** tab. To delete all history items click the **Delete** button in the **Internet Options** box, which will release the hard disc space used.

Fig. 4.24 General Internet Options.

Using Web Feeds

Web feeds (feeds for short) are usually used for news and blogs and contain frequently updated content published by a Web site. You can use feeds if you want updates to a Web site to be automatically downloaded to your PC.

When you visit a Web page that contains feeds, the grey **Feeds** button on the Internet Explorer toolbar changes to orange. To look at the feeds, click the feed symbol. To get content automatically downloaded to your computer, you will need to subscribe to the feed. This is very easy to do, and doesn't cost anything! Just tapping or clicking a **Subscribe to this feed** link, like that shown in Fig. 4.25, opens the **Subscribe to this Feed** box shown in Fig. 4.26.

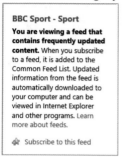

Fig. 4.25 Subscribing to a Web Feed.

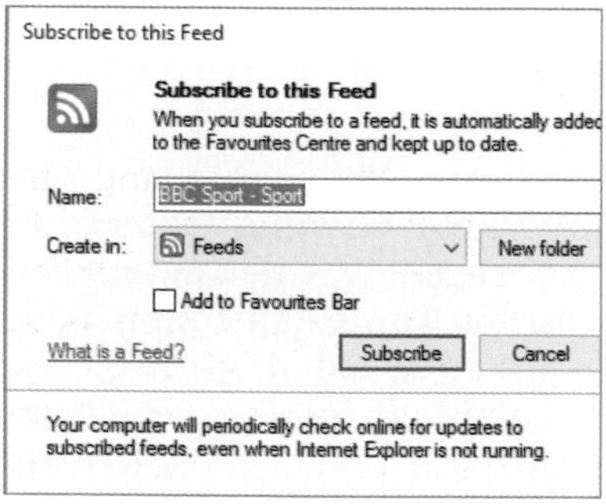

Fig. 4.26 Subscribe to this Feed Box.

Clicking the **Subscribe** button adds the feed to the 'Common Feed List' in the **Favourites Centre**, and updated information from the feed will be automatically down-loaded to your computer for viewing in **Internet Explorer**.

All your subscribed feeds will be listed in the **Feeds** section of the **Favourites Centre**. Selecting an item in the **Feeds** list, shown in Fig. 4.27, will open it in the main **Explorer** pane so you can keep up to date.

Fig. 4.27 Feeds List.

Tabbed Browsing

With tabbed browsing you can open several Web sites in one **Explorer** window each in its own tab, and switch between them by clicking on their tab. To create a new tab, tap or click the **New Tab** icon , pointed to in Fig. 4.28, immediately to the right of the existing tabs.

Fig. 4.28 Creating a New Tab.

Selecting the **New tab** icon, displays an empty address box in which you'll have to type a new address.

Fig. 4.29 The New Bing Page Tab.

So simply type a new Web address or use the **Favourites** button or select **Favourites** from the **Menu** bar and open one of your **Favourites**.

Explorer 11 retains the **InPrivate Browsing** mode of its predecessor which is opened by selecting **Tools** in the **Menu** bar, as shown in Fig. 4.30. Selecting it, opens a new window with information about the **InPrivate** mode and also informs you that it has been turned on. You can now safely browse without leaving any traces. Just closing the **InPrivate** window returns you to standard mode.

Fig. 4.30 The Tools Menu Bar Options.

Saving and Opening a Group of Tabs

To save a group of tabs so that you can open the pages again, do the following: Open the Web sites you want to save, maybe ones with a common theme. Tap or click the **Favourites** ⭐ button to open the **Favourites Center**, then click the down-arrow ▾ button by the **Add to Favourites** box, and select **Add Current Tabs to Favourites** from the drop-down list.

In the displayed dialogue box give a name to the folder to contain the selected Web sites – I called it **Best Buys**, (Fig. 4.31) and click the **Add** button.

Fig. 4.31 The Add Tabs to Favourites Box.

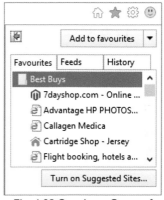

Fig. 4.32 Opening a Group of Tabs.

To open saved grouped Web sites, click the **Favourites** ⭐ button, select the **Favourites** option and choose a group of sites you want to open (perhaps something similar to what is shown in Fig. 4.32). Finally, tap or click the particular Web site you want to see to open it in the **Explorer**.

Changing Your Search Engine

You could change which Internet search engine you are using, if you are not happy with **bing**. For example, to change to **Google**, type **www.google.co.uk** in the **Address** bar (see Fig. 4.33) and either press the **Enter** key on the keyboard or tap/click the **Go to** → button to the right of the **Address** bar to open **Google**'s UK search page, as shown below.

Fig. 4.33 The Google Search Engine.

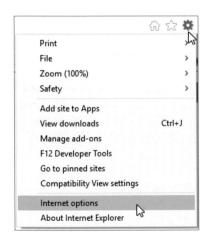

To make **Google** your default search engine, click the **Tools** ⚙ icon (pointed to at the top-right corner in Fig. 4.34), to open the **Tools** menu shown here. Next, tap or click the **Internet options** entry (also pointed to in Fig. 4.34), to open the multi-tab dialogue box shown in Fig. 4.35 on the next page.

Fig. 4.34 The Tools Menu.

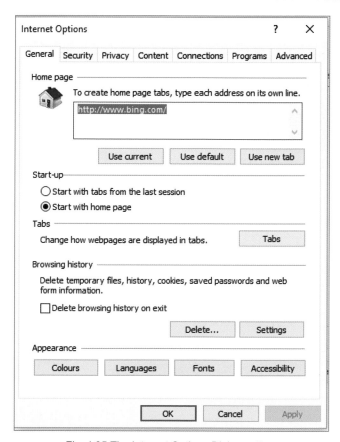

Fig. 4.35 The Internet Options Dialogue Box.

All you have to do now is replace the entry in the **Home page** text box with **www.google.co.uk/** and click the **Use current** button, followed by the **OK** button. From now on, whenever you tap or click on the **Internet Explorer** icon or tile, you will be displaying the **Google** UK page.

Note: As this book is about Microsoft's Windows 10, I'll continue with the Microsoft search engine. Therefore, in what follows, I'll continue using **bing**.

Internet Explorer Help

You can get help with **Explorer** by tapping or clicking the **Help**  button at the extreme right of the **Toolbar** or **Help** on the **Menu** bar and selecting the **Internet Explorer Help** entry from the drop-down menu of options shown in Fig. 4.36.

Fig. 4.36 Getting Help with Internet Explorer.

This displays the **Internet Explorer Help** screen showing various topics.

You can work your way through the items listed on the left of the displayed screen at your leisure. As you tap or click each such item, it opens a screen of links appropriate to that option, as shown in Fig. 4.37. Do try some of these.

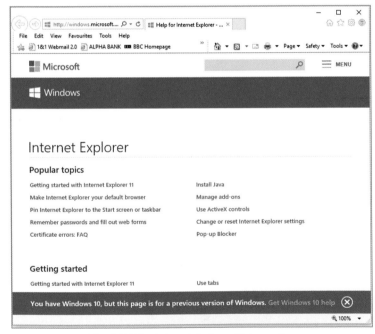

Fig. 4.37 The Internet Options Dialogue Box.

5

Mail, Contacts & Calendar

These three Apps are far more integrated in Windows 10 than in earlier versions of the Operating System.

For example, when I accessed **Calendar** for the first time, the screen in Fig. 5.1 was displayed.

Fig. 5.1 The Calendar Welcoming Screen.

Tapping or clicking the **Get started** button, displayed the screen in Fig. 5.2.

Fig. 5.2 The Accounts Screen.

Note that the App found two preexisting e-mail accounts and displayed them, and is ready to add more. You might wonder why **Calendar** should need to know an e-mail account, but the interaction between **Mail**, **Calendar** and **People** (otherwise known as **Contacts**) is very tight.

For example, you need a contact to send an e-mail to and, if you are organising a meeting with some people, you need to know when you are free and send them an invite by e-mail. Some of these topics will be discussed in more detail later on in the book.

The E-mail App

Windows 10 comes with a **Mail** App, the tile of which is to be found on the **Start** screen. It is a similar program to the one in Windows **Live Essentials**. The App is designed to work with Windows 10 very well and as long as you are connected to the Internet and set up correctly, you can communicate with others by e-mail wherever they are in the world, all you need to know is their e-mail address. In this section of the chapter, I look at Windows **Mail**, but you can also use different programs if you prefer.

Connecting to Your Server

If you already have a **Live** or **Gmail** account, then the **Mail** App will detect it, if not, then when you start **Mail** for the first time, you will be prompted to add one. You will need the following information from the supplier of your e-mail service:

- Your e-mail address and password
- The type of e-mail server to be used
- The address of the incoming and outgoing e-mail servers you should use.

If the connection process does not start automatically, use the **Settings** ⚙ button, pointed to in Fig. 5.3 on the next page.

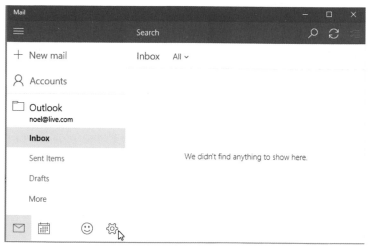

Fig. 5.3 The Windows Mail Screen.

Tapping or clicking the **Settings** button, opens the **Setting** window and superimposes it on the **Mail** screen, but shown separately in Fig. 5.4 below.

Next, select the **Accounts** option to display Fig. 5.5. Activating the **Add an account** option, displays the screen shown in Fig. 5.6.

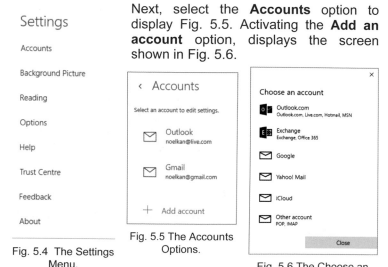

Fig. 5.4 The Settings Menu.

Fig. 5.5 The Accounts Options.

Fig. 5.6 The Choose an Account Options.

As you can see in Fig. 5.6, you have a number of choices of Internet-based accounts, but if you have an Internet-based account that is not listed or you need to add an account based on a Website, then you can choose the **Other account POP, IMAP** option.

You can add all your different e-mail accounts by following the same procedure so you can view them all from the same window. Once your connection is established, opening the **Inbox** will display any messages waiting in the mailbox of a specified account. Unfortunately in the **Mail** App, if you have more than one e-mail account, you have to cycle through them to see the messages in each account, as shown in Fig. 5.7. .

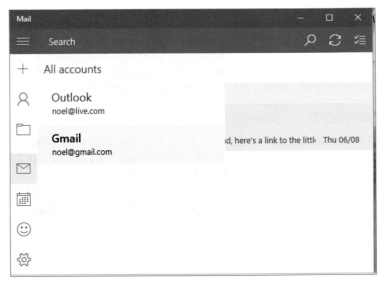

Fig. 5.7 The Windows Mail Screen.

The above display shows all existing accounts when the **Accounts** ⍺ button is tapped or clicked on the Windows **Mail** screen. A partially hidden e-mail sent to the currently selected (**Gmail**) account can be seen to the right of the screen. To see the full e-mail, tap or click the relevant account.

To see all your mail folders, tap or click the **All Folder**  option on the left of the **Mail** screen, to display the screen in Fig. 5.8.

The list contains folders, such as **Outbox**, **Inbox**, **Deleted items**, **Drafts**, **Junk**, and **Sent**. Tapping or clicking one of these, displays its contents. Selecting a message in the list, opens it so you can read it.

Before explaining in more detail other features of Windows **Mail**, I will step through the procedure of sending a very simple e-mail message. The best way to test out any unfamiliar e-mail features is to send a test message to your own e-mail address. This saves wasting somebody else's time, and the message can be checked very quickly. In fact, this is what was done above.

Fig. 5.8 The Folders List.

A Test E-mail Message

To start a test message, touch or click the **New** + button at the top-left corner of the screen shown in Fig. 5.8 to open the **New Message** window, shown in Fig. 5.9.

Fig. 5.9 Preparing a Test Message.

Do open this screen on your PC and size its width until all the text formatting tools are revealed as shown above. The formatting tools collapse, one by one, as the width of the window is made smaller and smaller.

Next, type your own e-mail address in the **To** field, and a title for the message in the **Subject** field which will form a header for the message when it is received, so it helps to show in a few words what the message is about.

Now, type your own text in the field above the signature '**Sent from Mail for Windows 10**' (known as the **Message** field, as shown above. I simply typed 'Testing mail' in the **Subject** field and 'My first e-mail message' in the **Message** field, although you might like to type a longer message.

If you make any mistake and want to correct or delete a word, or move words to another part of the message, then

On a touch sensitive screen:

- Touch and hold on the word you want to change (which highlights it and places movable handles under it) then select **Cut** from the displayed sub-menu `Cut | Copy | Paste | ⌄` options and retype the word.

- To move a number of words to another part of the message, touch and hold the first word then drag with your finger the movable handles to select all the words you want to move, choose **Cut** or **Copy** then move to where you want to insert the selected words and use the **Paste** option.

On a PC with a keyboard:

- Double-click the word you want to change (which highlights it) then retype the word.

- To move a number of words to another part of the message, place the cursor at the beginning of the first word and while holding down the left mouse key, drag the mouse pointer to select all the words you want to move, then use the key combination **Ctrl+X** (while holding down the **Control** key, press the **X** key on the keyboard) which removes the selected words from their current place (**Ctrl+C** copies the selection) then move to where you want to insert the selected words and use the key combination **Ctrl+V**.

If you tap or click the ↶ undo button, it removes the last character you typed or the word(s) you **Cut** or removed from your text, while the ↷ redo button reverses these changes. As for text formatting, size of font, etc., I leave it to you to experiment with and find out what suits you best.

If you tap or click on the **Discard** 🗑 button at the top right of the screen, the whole e-mail will be removed. To send the e-mail on its way, tap or click the **Send** ▷ button.

By default, your message is placed in the **Outbox** folder and sent immediately if you are on Broadband. When **Mail** next checks for e-mail messages, it should find the message and download it into your **Inbox** folder.

Cc to the right of the recipient's e-mail address in Fig. 5.9 (page 79), stands for 'carbon copy'. Anyone listed in the **Cc** field of a message receives a copy of that message when you send it. All other recipients of that message can see that the person you designated as a **Cc** recipient received a copy of the message.

Bcc stands for 'blind carbon copy'. **Bcc** recipients are invisible to all the other recipients of the message (including other **Bcc** recipients).

Replying to a Message

When you receive an e-mail message that you want to reply to, like the one shown in Fig. 5.10, **Mail** makes it very easy to do.

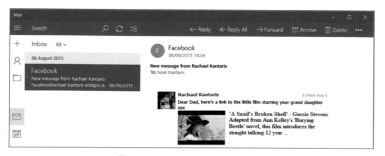

Fig. 5.10 A Received Message.

Provided you tap or click on a received e-mail to open it in the **Read Message** pane and the **Mail** window is sufficiently large enough, options to **Reply**, **Forward**, etc., display at the top of the **Read Message** pane.

To reply to such a message, tap or click the **Reply** option. The reply address and the new message subject fields are both added automatically for you. Also, by default, the original message is quoted in the reply window for you to edit as required.

As you can see, you can **Reply** only to the person who sent you the message, or to all the people who received the message. The **Forward** option is used to forward the message to another person altogether, in which case you'll have to supply their e-mail address.

Using E-mail Attachments

To add an attachment to an e-mail message, such as a photo or work file, simply start a new e-mail or reply to one, then tap or click the **Insert** tab at the top of the **Mail** screen, as shown in Fig. 5.11 below.

Fig. 5.11 The Insert Tab Options.

Tapping or clicking the **Pictures** tab, **Mail** assumes that you are about to attach a picture so it displays all your photos in your **Pictures** folder. If, next time you select the **Attach** option, **Mail** assumes that you want to attach the same type of attachment as before and will display the contents of your **Pictures** folder. However, if you were intending to attach a document file instead, you should navigate to your **Documents** folder and select one from there.

As an example, I attached three photos from my **Pictures** folder, and one file from my **Document**s folder, as shown in Fig. 5.12 on the next page, prior to sending the e-mail.

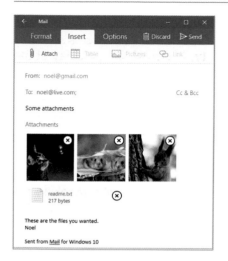

All you have to do now is send the e-mail, perhaps to yourself, so you can see and check the result.

Fig. 5.12 An E-mail Message with Attached Photos and a Text File.

Receiving Attachments

Fig. 5.13 below, shows the e-mail you'll receive with its attachments had you sent it to yourself.

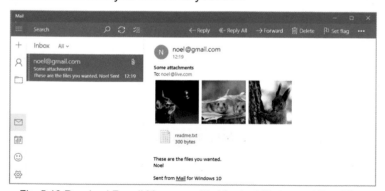

Fig. 5.13 Received E-mail Message with Attached Photos and Text File.

The received message shows the three pictures together with the attached (named) text file and its size. If you touch and hold or right-click each attachment, a pop-up menu displays inviting you to **Open** or **Save** the particular item. If you choose to save such attachments, do so into appropriate folders – save photos in **Pictures** and files in **Documents**.

Deleting Messages

Some e-mail messages you receive will be worth keeping, but most will need deleting. From the **Read Message** pane you just tap or click the ⊞ Delete button to do this. Whenever you delete a message it is moved to the **Deleted Items** folder.

Sending an E-mail to the Drafts Folder

If you decide that your e-mail is not complete yet and further changes are needed before sending it, simply open another e-mail. The very act of doing so, sends the unfinished e-mail to the **Drafts** folder, but it also remains in the **Inbox** marked as **Draft**. This allows you to retrieve it later for further editing.

Summary of System Folders

The number and exact name of folders available in **Mail** depend on which account you are using. To see these, tap or click the **Folders** option on the **Folders** list. Most of these have been discussed already, but here is a summary of their function.

- The **Inbox** holds all incoming messages. These can be moved or copied into any other folder except the **Outbox** folder.

- The **Outbox** folder holds messages that have been prepared but not yet transmitted. As soon as the messages are sent they are automatically removed to the **Sent** folder.

- The **Sent** folder holds messages that have been transmitted. You can then decide whether to 'file' copies of these messages, or whether to delete them. Messages in the **Sent** folder can be moved or copied into any of the other folders except the **Outbox** folder.

- The **Deleted Items** folder holds messages that have been deleted and placed in there as a safety feature. Messages in the **Deleted Items** folder can be moved into any of the other folders, except the **Outbox** folder.

- The **Drafts** folder is used to hold a message you started and then tried doing something else. Messages in the **Drafts** folder cannot be moved or copied into any of the other folders. Simply tap or click such a message to open it, edit it, and then send it.

- The **Junk** folder (also referred to as **Spam** by some e-mail accounts) is designed to catch unsolicited messages.

To **Move** an e-mail from one folder to another, touch and hold or right-click it to display the folders to move it to.

Printing Messages

Occasionally you might receive an important e-mail message that you would like to print and file for safe keeping. This is very easy to do. First, display the e-mail you want to print on your computer's screen, then tap or click the **Actions** button to display the menu shown in Fig. 5.14. Choosing the **Print** option, displays the screen in Fig. 5.15 in which you can select a printer, page layout, etc.

Fig. 5.14 The Actions Menu.

Fig. 5.15 The Printer Screen.

Note: What prints is only the actual e-mail, not the attachments which must be saved and printed separately.

The People App

Windows **Mail** lets you create and keep a list of **People** (also called 'contacts') to store details such as the names, addresses, phone numbers and e-mail addresses of all those you communicate with most.

If you have upgraded to Windows 10, your 'contacts' would have automatically been transferred across. Your **People** list will contain the contacts you have added or imported into the program from mail accounts you add to Windows **Mail**. If you add **Live Mail** or **Gmail** into Windows **Mail**, then the 'contacts' list associated with these services will be transported across.

If the **People** App is not pinned to the **Start** menu, tap or click the **All apps** ⊞ All apps button at the bottom of the **Start** menu, then find it ■ in the displayed list of Apps, touch and hold or right-click its entry and select the option to **Pin to Start** from the pop-up menu, so it can be easily accessible.

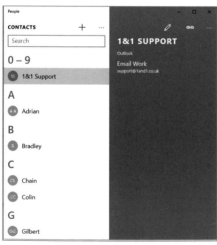

Fig. 5.16 Part of the People List.

If all is well, selecting the **People** App on the **Start** screen, should change your screen to one similar to that in Fig. 5.16.

Note that when you select the **0 - 9** entry in Fig. 5.16, the screen changes to display the alphabet so that you can jump to any part of the list quickly and easily by simply tapping or clicking the required letter.

To preserve anonymity, I have removed the surnames of my contacts in the above list.

On the top right corner of a contact's details screen, you can

Fig. 5.17.

see three buttons. When you tap of click the **See more** ■ button (the one at the extreme right of the group), two things happen: (i) labels appear under the other two, namely **Edit** and **Link** and (ii) an additional menu displays below the area, as shown in Fig. 5.17.

Selecting the **Share contact** option, opens a pane in which you insert the e-mail address of the person you want to share the selected contact, while choosing the **Delete** option, deletes the contact in question, although touching and holding or right clicking a contact gives you a quicker option to edit or delete it. Details of a contact can be changed or added to, using the **Edit** button, while the **Link** button allows you to link multiple profiles of a selected person.

You can add a new contact, as shown in Fig. 5.18, by selecting the **Add** + button at the top of the contacts list, as shown in Fig. 5.16 on the previous page.

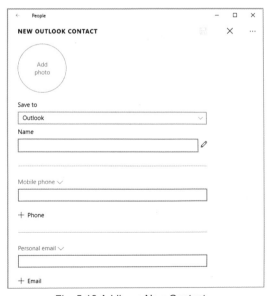

Fig. 5.18 Adding a New Contact.

You can select the account in which to save the new contact, for example **Outlook** or **Gmail**, etc., enter the name, phone and e-mail details for your new contact. Personal information can be entered now or later by editing the contact's entry. Once all is done, tap or click the **Save** ▣ button.

The Settings Options

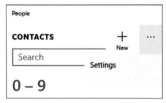

Fig. 5.19 The See More Menu.

Tap of click the **See more** ⋯ button, the one at the top of the **Contacts** pane, shown here in Fig. 5.19, and tap or click the displayed **Settings** option to open the screen in Fig. 5.20.

Fig. 5.20 The Settings Screen.

The **Settings** screen can be used to **Add an account** which might hold more contacts, such as one kept in **OneDrive** and specify how the list of contacts should display. I personally prefer to have my list of contacts sorted by **First Name**, as shown Fig. 5.20 on the previous page, but if there are too many people with the same first name, then within that group, I choose by **First name** then by **Surname**.

Sending Messages Using the Contacts List

To send a new e-mail message using the **Contacts** list, open **Mail**, and in the **To:** field, type the first few letters of the name to whom you want to send an e-mail. As you are typing, a list of suggestions appears below the **To:** field, of people in your **Contacts** list, as shown in Fig. 5.21.

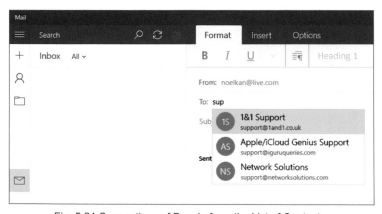

Fig. 5.21 Suggestions of People from the List of Contacts.

As you type more characters, the suggested contacts shrink in number. Once you see what you are looking for, simply tap or click the correct suggestion and then write the rest of the e-mail. This method can be used with new and forwarded e-mail messages - it saves a lot of time!

The Calendar App

The Windows 10 **Start** screen also provides you with a **Calendar** tile which when you tap or click, opens the screen shown in Fig. 5.22.

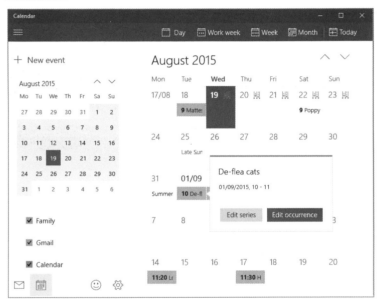

Fig. 5.22 The Opened Calendar.

You can create two types of entries in **Calendar** – events that only occur once (such as having lunch with a friend) and reoccurring events (such as birthdays). Tapping or clicking on a reoccurring entry displays the message **Edit series** or **Edit occurrence**, as shown in Fig. 5.22 above. To edit this event and all future events, select **Edit series**, while if you want to only edit the current event without changing the rest of the series, select **Edit occurrence**.

To create a new event, tap or click on a free day on the **Calendar**, where no events have been scheduled already, to open the screen shown in Fig. 5.23 on the next page. Do try to create a test entry – you can always delete it afterwards.

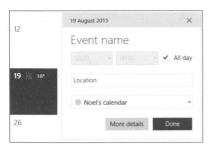

Fig. 5.23 Creating a New Event.

First, give the event a name and if it doesn't occupy the whole day, remove the tick against **All day** and give the event a starting and ending time in the two grey oblongs.

To add additional details to the event, tap or click the **More details** button to open a screen similar to that in Fig. 5.24, in which you can set a **Reminder**, specify if this entry is a **Repeat** event or not and whether you want to **Invite someone** from your contacts list to attend.

Fig. 5.24 Creating a Calendar Entry.

Fig. 5.25 Inviting a Person.

If you decide to invite some people to attend, say, for a meeting, then tap or click the **Invite someone** box and type the first few characters of the name of the person you want to invite. Just as with the creation of e-mail messages, as you type, suggestions appear of people's e-mail addresses from your contacts list. The more characters you type the fewer the displayed suggestions.

You could, of course, invite more that one person to your meeting, just as you could send the same e-mail to more than one person.

Once you have completed all the entries you need, tap or click the **Save and close** button at the top of the screen (see Fig. 5.26 below). If, however, you tap or click the **Return** to **Calendar** button instead, a pop-up message displays asking you to choose between **Save** or **Discard changes** as shown in Fig. 5.26.

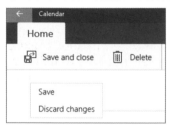

A saved event can always be deleted by opening it, then tap or click the **Delete** 🗑 Delete button.

Fig. 5.26 Exiting an Event.

In Fig. 5.22 (page 90), **Calendar** is displayed in monthly view. Instead, you could choose to display events in **Day**, **Work week** or **Week** view by tapping or clicking one of the options at the top of an opened **Calendar** screen.

Finally, you might have noticed some symbols displaying against certain days, as shown in Fig. 5.27 below. These show rain, sun and cloud, etc.

Thursday	Friday	Saturday	Sunday
20 🌧 18° / 15°	21 🌧 17° / 14°	22 🌧 17° / 12°	23 🌥 15° / 12°

Fig. 5.27 Weather Forecast Information and links.

Tapping of clicking one of these symbols, the ones nearest to the date (which in reality are links to a Web site), opens the Web site in **Explorer** and gives you more detailed weather information.

It is worth spending sometime exploring **Calendar** and its excellent facilities. You'll never again forget someone's birthday or an appointment!

6

Photos, Videos & Music

In Windows 10, you can either use the **Photos** tile provided on the **Start** screen to access your photos and videos in a collage-type format (more likely appreciated by tablet users) or via the **This PC** tile which allows access to the individual folders containing your **Photos**, **Videos** and **Music** (more likely used by desktop and laptop users).

The Photos App

 Clicking the **Photos** tile on the **Start** screen, displays the screen shown in Fig. 6.1 below. Do note, however, that the picture on the **Photos** App tile shown to the left, changes because the photos in the **Pictures** folder of **My PC** (more about this later) are shown as a live slide show, therefore what is shown here is bound to be different for you.

Fig. 6.1 Photos Displayed by the Photos App.

There are two areas on the screen in Fig. 6.1 that need to be discussed. First, lets have a look at the left of the screen which displays what is shown in Fig. 6.2.

At the very top left of the screen, tapping or clicking the left-pointing ← arrow takes you back to the view of Fig. 6.1, shown on the previous page, from wherever you happen to be in the **Photos** options – which displays your photos in **Collection** 🖼 view.

The three horizontal lines ☰ button is the **Menu**. Tapping or clicking the **Menu** button changes the view of your photos from **Collection** to **Albums** 🖼 and back again.

The first of the two buttons at the bottom left of your screen is your account (in this case associated with my 🔵 **live.com** account), while the **Settings** ⚙ button displays a screen in which you can select your **Viewing and editing** options. I leave it to you to investigate this screen.

Fig. 6.2.

On the top right of the screen in Fig. 6.1 (shown on the previous page) you'll see a group of buttons, as shown in Fig. 6.3.

The labels under the first three buttons only appear if you tap or click the **See more** ⋯ button at the extreme right of the group.

Fig. 6.3.

The **Refresh** button starts a search for any extra photos you might have added to your collection since the last refresh. The **Select** button places small squares at the top right of each photo allowing the selection of the ones you want to **Share**, **Copy** or **Delete**, using the buttons in Fig. 6.4. The buttons in Fig. 6.4, replace those in Fig. 6.3. Again the labels under them only appear if you tap or click the **See more** ⋯ button at the extreme right of the new group.

Fig. 6.4.

Using the **Import**  button in Fig. 6.3 requires a device such a camera, a memory stick or card to be connected to your computer via a USB (short for Universal Serial Bus) port. If no such device is found, the **Photos** App displays the message in Fig. 6.5.

Tapping or clicking on a photo, displays even further buttons at the top right of the screen, as shown in Fig. 6.6 below.

Connect a device
Connect the device that you want to import from, and make sure that it's turned on and unlocked.

Try again   Close

Fig. 6.5 Warning Message.

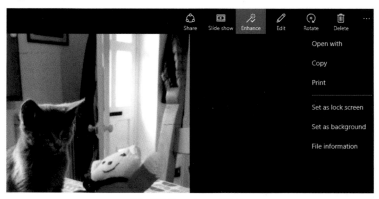

Fig. 6.6 Opening a Photo.

Again the labels under the various buttons only appear if you tap or click the **See more** ▪▪▪ button at the extreme right of the group. Using these buttons (from left to right) you can **Share** the selected picture via **Mail** or **Social Jogger** – **Facebook**, **Tweeter** or **You Tube**, start a **Slide show** or **Enhance** the picture with one touch or click.

The **Edit** button gives you a large number of editing tools which you can use to **Crop** or **Straighten** a picture, correct **Red eye** or add **Filters**, **Light**, **Colour** and **Effects**. The last two buttons allow you to **Rotate** or **Delete** a picture. Finally, from the **See more** drop-down menu you can use the **Open with** option to edit a photo in **Paint** or **Windows Photo Viewer**, **Copy**, **Print** or **Set as lock screen** or **background**.

Obviously, you could spend quite a bit of time here!

The Desktop Pictures Folder

If you upgraded to Window 10 and selected to keep your data and programs, you'll find that your photos are to be found in the **Pictures** folder which then is the default location for saving pictures and importing them from your digital camera.

To find this folder, tap or click **This PC** tile on the **Start** menu, shown here, to open the screen in Fig. 6.7 below. Note that in the address box below, the entry **My PC** displays when you used **This PC** tile – it opens my personal photos!

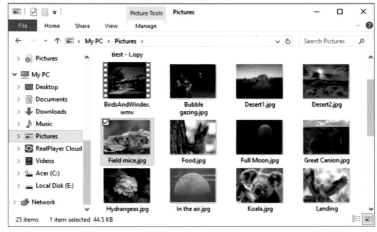

Fig. 6.7 The My PC Folders.

As you can see above, there are folders under **My PC** for **Documents**, **Downloads**, **Music**, **Pictures** and **Videos**. I keep most images I like in the (default) **Pictures** folder, but keep my personal photos in sub-folders in another location on my hard drive.

The Picture Tools

In Fig. 6.7, the **Ribbon** is minimised. Expanding the **Ribbon** reveals tools that are mostly greyed out until a picture is selected. When that is done, then you can **Delete** the selected picture, **Rename** it, **Move** it, **Copy** it, etc.

Fig. 6.8 shows the tools available to you on the **Ribbon** when a picture is selected and the **Picture Tools** button is tapped or clicked. You can now **Rotate** the selected picture to the left or right, **Set** it as background, or start a **Slide show**.

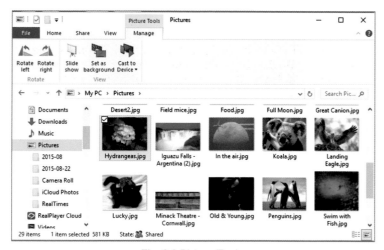

Fig. 6.8 Picture Tools.

Other **Ribbon** options allow you to **Share** selected pictures with friends and family, as was discussed earlier. It might be worth spending some time here, going through the various **Toolbar** options, to discover for yourself what is available.

The Windows Photo Viewer

To see a larger view of a picture, touch and hold or right-click it to open a contextual menu, then choose the **Open with** option to display a further menu similar to that in Fig. 6.9.

Fig. 6.9 Program Options.

Selecting the **Windows Photo Viewer**, displays the photo as shown in Fig. 6.10 on the next page. The **Toolbar** at the top offers **File** options, **Print**, **E-mail**, or **Burn** the selected photo to a data disc or **Open** a photo for viewing or possibly editing.

Fig. 6.10 The Windows Photo Viewer.

You can use the controls at the bottom of the **Viewer** to navigate through the current folder, view the pictures in your folder as a slide show, zoom in or out, rotate the image, and delete it from your hard disc.

Printing Photos

Selecting a picture in the **Viewer** and tapping or clicking the **Print** option, displays Fig. 6.11 below.

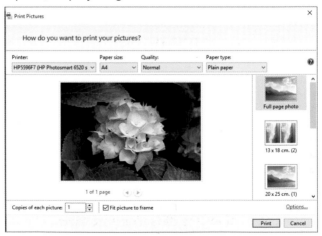

Fig. 6.11 The Print Pictures Window.

From here you can select the **Printer** to be used, **Paper size**, **Quality** of print, **Paper Type** and a variety of layouts for your pictures. All you have to do then is tap or click the **Print** button.

Using the **Ribbon**, you can **Delete**, **Copy**, or **Rename** a selected picture, or by using the **Picture Tools** option, shown open in Fig. 6.12, you can **Rotate**, **Set as background**, **Cast to Device** or start a **Slide show**.

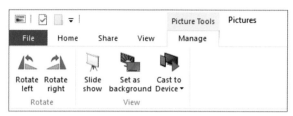

Fig. 6.12 The Set of Picture Tools.

To exit from the **Photos** App, tap or click the upwards pointing arrow, shown selected in Fig. 6.13 below.

Fig. 6.13 The Set of Picture Tools.

This has the effect of moving you up the folder's structure tree 'one level' and taking you to the screen showing **My PC** (see Fig. 6.7 on page 96).

The left pointing arrow has the effect of moving you back to the level on the structure tree you were just before you used the upward pointing arrow (in this case back to the **Pictures** folder), while the right pointing arrow moves you forward to the place in the folder structure tree you were before using the left pointing arrow.

It is extremely useful to understand how to get to a file within a folder which itself might be within another folder in a treelike structure of folders. It is similar to looking for a letter, which is in a folder, in a draw, of a particular filing cabinet.

Getting Photos from a Device

Windows 10 makes the process of importing pictures from your digital camera or phone to your computer extremely simple.

Once you have taken some photos, connect the camera or phone to your computer with the appropriate USB cable and turn the device on, which causes its automatic detection. In this case the device is my iPhone and a pop up is displayed, similar to that in Fig. 6.14 below. Tapping or clicking the **Import photos and videos** (**Photos**) option, starts importing the photos and videos from the device to the **Pictures** folder.

Microsoft hasn't quite decided what the name of the folder where photos are sent should be called. In previous versions of Windows it was consistently called **Pictures**, but in Windows 10 the name is interchangeable with **Photos**!

Fig. 6.14 About to Start the Import Process from a Portable Device.

The other displayed options above, allow you to send your photos from the connected device to **OneDrive**, to another folder on your PC (other than **Pictures**) or to your **Phone Companion**.

The imported photos are sent to a sub-folder within the **Pictures** folder, as shown in Fig. 6.15 on the next page. You can see this by using the **File Explorer** on the **Desktop**.

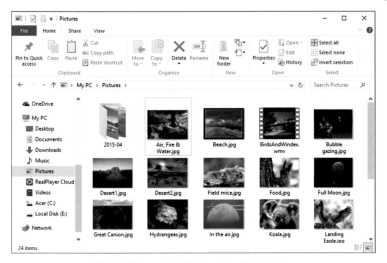

Fig. 6.15 Imported Photos in a Sub-folder.

Each photo in the folder is given a number which depends on your device. If you are happy with this, fine. If not you can spend a while renaming the folder and each picture.

If you are like me and you don't import your photos into your computer often enough, then this is the time to use the desktop **File Explorer** to create new folders with appropriate names and sort your photos now rather than later, as it is very easy to forget where each photo was taken and when!

Scanning Photos

To import the images from paper photographs or slides into your computer you have to use a scanner. These are fairly cheap these days, in fact many printers include the ability to scan, copy, as well as print. To handle slides effectively though you need a special slide and negative scanner, but be warned these are not cheap! Instead it would be more sensible to use the services of a specialist shop.

Using the Windows Scan Facility

There are many ways to control a scanner using third party software, but Windows 10 comes with its own program called **Windows Scan**, which you can only access from the **Control Panel**.

With your scanner properly installed and turned on, touch and hold or right-click the **Start** button, then selecting the **Control Panel** from the displayed menu, in Fig. 6.16.

This opens the **Control Panel** screen in Fig. 6.17 in which you select **View devices and printers** in the **Hardware and Sound** group when in **Category** view. If **Control Panel** opens in **Large icons** view (see Fig. 2.25, page 29), select **Devices and Printers**.

Either of these displays a screen similar to that shown in Fig. 6.18 on the next page.

Programs and Features
Power Options
Event Viewer
System
Device Manager
Network Connections
Disk Management
Computer Management
Command Prompt
Command Prompt (Admin)

Task Manager
Control Panel
File Explorer
Search
Run

Shut down or sign out   >
Desktop

Fig. 6.16 The Start Menu Options.

Fig. 6.17 The Control Panel Items.

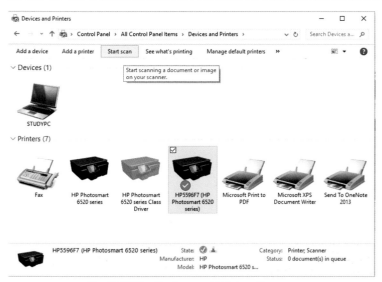

Fig. 6.18 The Devices and Printers Screen.

Tap or click the default printer (which happens to be an all-in-one type in my case) to open a menu of options at the top of the screen in Fig. 6.18 and select **Start scan** to open the screen shown in Fig. 6.19.

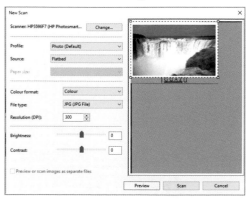

It is assumed that your photo is on the scanner before using the **Preview** option so that you can limit the actual scan to the correct size by dragging the handles of the cropping tool, as shown here.

Fig. 6.19 The Preview of the Scanned Photo.

Having done so, you can use the **Scan** button to start the actual scan and display the screen shown in Fig. 6.20 on the next page.

On this screen you can choose to **Review** or **Import** the scanned photo before pressing the **Next** button. Accepting the default setting and pressing the **Next** button, displays the screen shown

Fig. 6.20 The Import Pictures and Videos Screen.

in Fig. 6.21 where you can enter a name, add a tag, etc., before finally importing it into its own folder available in the **Pictures** library.

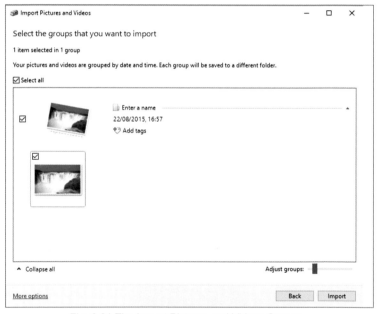

Fig. 6.21 The Import Pictures and Videos Screen.

The **Windows Scan** facility is not particularly intuitive, but it is easy enough to work with once you find out how to do it. The folder created and available to the **Pictures** library is similar to that created when you import pictures from a camera.

The Desktop Videos Folder

If you upgraded to Window 10 and selected to keep your data and programs, you'll find that your videos are to be found in the **Videos** folder which then is the default location for saving videos you might have received as attachments to e-mail messages, or imported from your video recorder.

If you did not upgrade as mentioned above, then the default folder were videos are saved would be the same as **Photos**. To find the **Videos** folder, tap or click the tile **This PC** on the **Start** menu and select **Video** to open the screen in Fig. 6.22.

Fig. 6.22 The Videos Folder.

The **Ribbon** tools are mostly greyed out until a video is selected. When that is done, then you can **Delete** the selected video, **Rename** it, **Move** it, **Copy** it, etc., while other **Ribbon** options allow you to **Share** selected videos.

The Video Tools

Tapping or clicking the **Video Tools** above the **Ribbon** in

Fig. 6.22, reveals additional tools that you can use with your videos, as shown here in Fig. 6.23.

Fig. 6.23 The Video Tools.

The Windows Video App

To start a video playing, double-tap or double-click it to open it in the **Film & TV** App, as shown in Fig. 6.24 below.

Fig. 6.24 The Film & TV App.

This video is of the **.wmv** (Windows Media Video) format and can also be opened in the **Windows Media Player**. To find this App, tap or click the **Start** button, then choose the **All apps** menu option and swipe up or scroll down to the **Windows** entries.

If you touch and hold or right-click a video, a menu of options is displayed, as shown in Fig. 6.25, in which the third option is **Play with Windows Media Player**. Try it to see which of the two players you prefer.

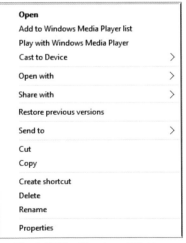

Fig. 6.25 The Touch and Hold or
Right-click Menu Options for a Video.

The Film & TV App

Next time you tap or click the **Film & TV** tile, shown here, you'll find that the App has been populated with all your videos – well, most of them, but in an easy way to find them, as shown in Fig. 6.26.

Fig. 6.26 The Contents of the Film & TV App.

As you can see, videos are displayed in alphabetical order and tapping or clicking the **0 – 9** options at the top of the screen, displays the alphabet so you can jump to the video you want, provided it is named and you know that name. There is also a search facility.

Next, tap or click the **Menu** ≡ button at the top of the screen and select **Settings** ⚙, then **Choose where we look for videos** from the sub-menu to display Fig. 6.27

Selecting the **Add** ➕ button, displays folders to choose from. In my case, I selected the **C:\Users\Noel\Videos** folder where all my personal photos and videos were kept. Now all my videos are in one place, namely in **Film & TV**.

Fig. 6.27 The Where to Look for Videos Screen.

The Desktop Music Folder

If you upgraded to Window 10 and selected to keep your data and programs, you'll find that your music collection is to be found in the **Music** folder which then is the default location for saving any music you might have downloaded, or imported from a CD.

To find the **Music** folder, tap or click the tile **This PC** on the **Start** menu and select **Music** to open the screen in Fig. 6.28

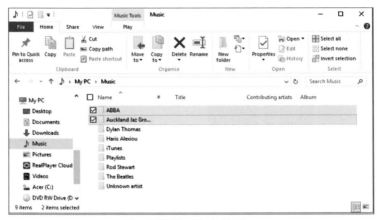

Fig. 6.28 The Music Folder.

Just as in the case of **Videos**, the **Ribbon** tools for **Music** are mostly greyed out until a track is selected. When that is done, then you can **Delete** the selected truck, **Rename** it, **Move** it, **Copy** it, etc., while other **Ribbon** options allow you to **Share** selected music tracks.

The Music Tools

Tapping or clicking the **Music Tools** above the **Ribbon** in

Fig. 6.28, reveals additional tools that you can use with your music, as shown here in Fig. 6.29.

Fig. 6.29 The Music Tools.

The Windows Music App

To start a music track playing, double-tap or double-click it. The first time you do this, it opens a window in which you are asked '**How do you want to open this file?**' The first choice offered is **Groove Music** which you can also make the default App to play such music.

Next time you tap or click on the **Groove Music** tile on the **Start** menu, you'll find that it has searched your PC and populate the App with music tracks as shown in Fig. 6.30.

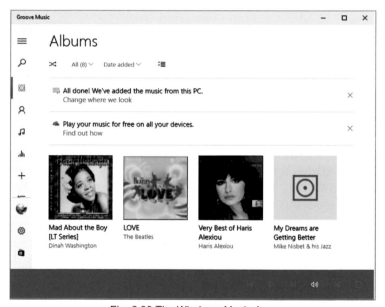

Fig. 6.30 The Windows Music App.

Unfortunately, all music tracks on your PC automatically load into the **Groove Music** App, including all Windows and video sounds! You could go through these and delete what you don't want, but the best way is to tap or click the **Change where we look** option, to be found near the top of the screen in Fig. 6.30, to display a screen similar to the one shown in Fig. 6.31 on the next page.

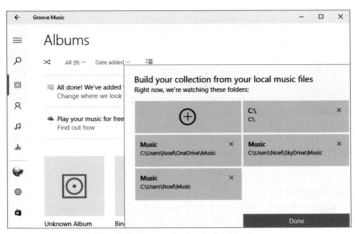

Fig. 6.31 Where to Look for Music.

I suggest you tap or click the **C:** drive and remove it from the list, as that is where all the Windows sounds are to be found. Then, transfer everything from **SkyDrive** to **OneDrive**, before removing the **SkyDrive** from the above list.

To do this, use **My PC** tile twice to open two windows and select **C:\Users**(YourName)**\SkyDrive** for one and the same, but **OneDrive** for the other, then select one item at a time on the **SkyDrive** and with your finger (or the **Shift** key depressed), drag it to the **OneDrive** (see Fig. 6.32).

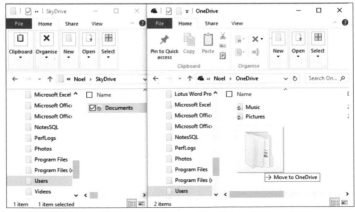

Fig. 6.32 Transferring Files from a Drive into a Different Drive.

The Desktop Windows Media Player

 You can use Windows **Media Player** to play the digital media files stored on your computer, or on CDs, or other external storage devices. It provides a good-looking, intuitive and easy-to-use interface.

You can organise your digital media collection, rip music from your CDs to the computer and burn CDs of your favourite music, so you can play them on other devices.

It also lets you sync (synchronise) digital media files to a large range of portable media devices and encourages you to buy digital media content online. With **Media Player** you can play your audio and video material, view it and organise it.

By default, the **Windows Media Player** is not pinned on the **Taskbar**, where it would be convenient to have it. So, the first thing to do is to go to the **All apps** option of the **Start** menu, swipe up or scroll down to **Windows Media Player** touch and hold or right-click it and select **Pin to taskbar** from the displayed menu. In this way you can start it a lot easier. Next, tap or click the **Windows Media Player** icon to open the program and if a CD is in your optical drive it will display its content and display a view similar to that in Fig. 6.33.

Fig. 6.33 A Player View of a Music CD.

If the **Media Player** does not recognise the CD automatically it will show as an **Unknown album**. It is usually easy to correct this by touching and holding or right-clicking the default album artwork graphic and selecting the **Find album info** option. The CD has to be an original, not a copy!

Ripping from Audio CDs

The tracks and songs on an inserted CD will not show in your **Library** unless you 'rip' them from the CD. This is not as destructive as it sounds. It simply means copying tracks from the CD to the library on your computer's hard disc, so that you can listen to them whenever it suits you.

By default, Windows **Media Player** rips to **.wma** format with CD quality encoding. This is good enough for me, but if you want to change these settings click **Rip settings** on the **Button** bar and choose **More options**.

The tracks ready to be ripped from the inserted audio CD (see Fig. 6.33 on previous page) display in the **Details** pane, ready to be copied to your library.

If there are any tracks that you don't want to rip, clear the check box next to them (Fig. 6.33). When you are ready, click the **Rip CD** button on the **Button** bar, shown here, to start the process. You will be warned about licence requirements, etc., after which ripping begins.

By default the selected tracks are copied to the **Music** library on your PC with folders added and labelled with the name of the artist or group.

While the ripping operation is in progress you can see exactly what is going on by looking at the **Rip status** column. You can listen to the CD while you are ripping it, so you needn't get too bored. By the time you listen to one track, the whole process would have completed.

To cancel ripping at any time, just tap or click the **Stop rip** button. Once you have ripped one CD you will find it very easy to rip your whole collection.

Player View Modes

Media Player lets you toggle between two main view modes. The **Player Library** shown in Fig. 6.34 below (which gives you control of all the **Player**'s features) and a **Now Playing** mode, shown in Fig. 6.35 (which gives a simplified view ideal for playback).

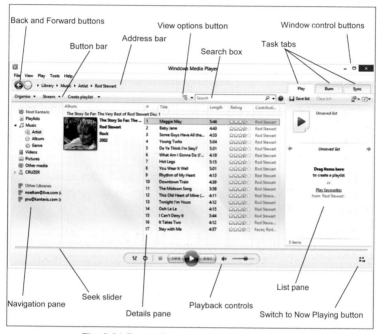

Fig. 6.34 Parts of the Player Library Window.

To move between these modes click the **Switch to Now Playing** button, or from the **Media Player**, the **Switch to Library** button in the upper-right corner pointed to in Fig. 6.35.

Fig. 6.35 Now Playing Mode.

When you tap or click an item, such as **Music**, in the **Navigation** pane, it lists your media content in the **Details** pane. Tapping or clicking on **Artist** will list your music files by artist and double-tapping or double-clicking on a CD icon, lists the tracks on that CD. Double-tapping or double-clicking on a track name will start it playing in the **Media Player**.

There are three different viewing options in the **Details** pane, chosen from a drop-down menu by tapping or clicking the arrow next to the **View options** button, shown here in Fig. 6.36, or by just tapping or clicking the button itself repeatedly until you get the view you want.

Fig.6.36 The View Options.

Searching a Library

When you want to find a specific artist, album title or song name, you can simply type a search string in the **Search** box as shown in Fig. 6.37. For example, typing **help** immediately presents results of the search (top-half of Fig. 6.37) and tapping or clicking on it, displays another screen with the actual details (bottom-half of Fig. 6.37) naming the **Beatles** album and the track number in this example.

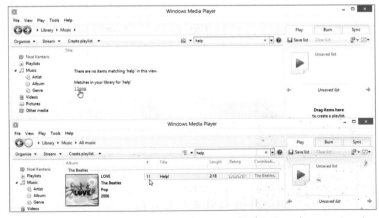

Fig. 6.37 Searching for Specific Music.

Double-tapping or double-clicking on the track number plays the song. It is that simple!

The **Playback Controls** are always visible at the bottom of the **Player Library** and their functions are similar to a normal CD player.

Burning CDs

With **Media Player** you can burn, or create, CD-R and CD-RW type CDs (read only or rewriteable ones), as long as you have a suitable recorder on your PC. To begin, insert a blank CD into your disc drive. If the **AutoPlay** window pops up, choose **Burn an audio CD using Windows Media Player**. If not simply open Windows **Media Player** as usual.

Fig. 6.38 The Burn List Pane.

You burn a CD in the **Burn List** pane shown in Fig. 6.38. This should appear automatically, but if it doesn't just tap or click the **Burn** tab.

If there are items in the list, click **Clear list** to remove them. To name the new disc tap or click the **Burn list** item pointed to in Fig. 6.38, and type a name for it. This will show up on CD players that support CD text.

As with a **Playlist**, to add songs to the **Burn** list, find them in your **Player Library** and drag and drop them into the new list.

If necessary you next choose the **Disc Type** you want to burn. There are three different types of discs you can burn:

Audio CD – These hold about 80 minutes of music, are readable by computers and are playable in any CD player. This type was automatically selected in the example above.

Data CD – These hold about 700 MB of data, are readable by computers and CD players that support playback of digital audio files. They are not playable on standard CD players.

Data DVD – These hold about 4 GB of data and are readable by DVD players that support playback of digital audio files. They are primarily intended to be readable by computers.

Windows DVD Player

> **Note:** In Windows 10, if you intend to play a film on your computer which is on a DVD disc, you need to install **Windows DVD Player**, which can be found in the **All apps** list of the **Start** button, before doing so.

To choose the type of disc to burn, click the **Burn options** button in the top right corner and select from the drop-down menu. You can also adjust other options by clicking **More burn options** which opens the **Media Player Options** box where you can choose various options.

When you are happy with your settings, tap or click **Apply**, then **OK**, followed by the **Start burn** button. When the burn begins, the status is shown in a green bar at the top of the **Burn List**. Tapping or clicking the blue text link below it, lets you see the status of each individual track.

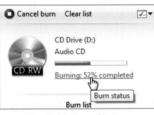

Fig. 6.39 Burn Status.

Quite a straightforward operation which you can use to create audio CDs to use in your car on those long boring journeys abroad!

> **Note:** You can use **Media Player** to look at your **Videos** and **Pictures**. The number of videos collected on my laptop are far greater than any other application. Try it and have fan!

7

Bing Maps

I hope you love maps as much as I do, because this chapter is dedicated to them. **Bing Maps** help you to see a 2D view of the world in **Road**, **Aerial**, **Bird's eye** and **Streetside**.

You can use **Bing Maps** to plan your holiday, search for locations and addresses, find local services, get driving or walking directions, or just to enjoy looking at maps in their various views, as they are available for all over the world. Its satellite imagery covers the entire planet, but at varying levels of resolution. You can approach **Bing Maps** either by activating the **Maps** tile on the **Start** screen or from the **Desktop**.

 Bing Maps is an example of 'cloud computing' as you view maps in a Web browser and everything is downloaded from the Internet. The maps load quickly, especially if a reasonably fast Broadband connection is available, otherwise a little patience might be needed!

The Maps App

If you tap or click the **Maps** App tile on the **Start** screen, what displays first is a map of your general location. Now, although I live in Cornwall and the map of Cornwall is shown, when I tap or click the **Show my location** on the displayed toolbar, shown in Fig. 7.1, the result is rather startling, as you can see in Fig. 7.2 on the next page.

Fig. 7.1 The Show my Location
Button on the Toolbar.

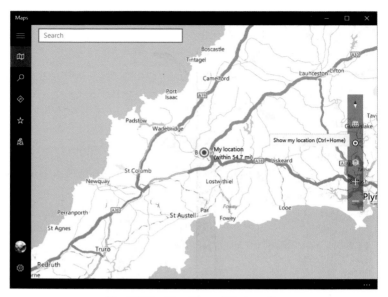

Fig. 7.2 The Map View of My Location.

My true location is near the bottom left corner of the above map, but the App puts me in North Cornwall, near Bodmin! Perhaps because there is no GPS on my PC? Pointing to that location, the caption **My location (within 54.7 miles)** is displayed, but there is no way of providing my true location!

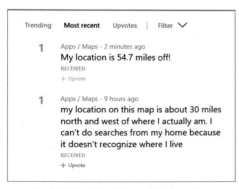

Fig. 7.3 The Map View of My Location.

The three dots at the bottom right corner of the map in Fig. 7.2 allow you to send **Feedback** to the designers of the App and see other peoples' posts. The most recent posts, including mine, at the time of writing are shown in Fig. 7.3.

Next, I tried to get directions by providing my postcode as the starting point and Redruth (the nearest town) as the destination. The result is shown in Fig. 7.4.

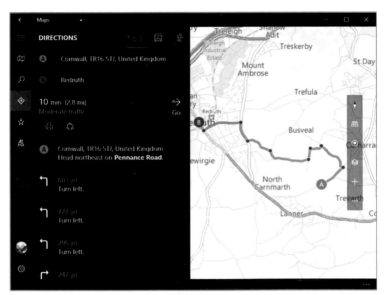

Fig. 7.4 The Suggested Wrong Route from A to B.

The suggested route (by turning Northeast) then heading up the Carn (hill in Cornish) via narrow roads (shown in blue), is positively the wrong way! Instead, by turning in the opposite direction at the starting point (Southwest), one can join the main road (shown in green) straight into Redruth!

This did not give me confidence and it would seem more work is needed on this App!

The Desktop Bing Maps Environment

Once your browser is opened and **Bing** is your search engine, click the **Maps** option at the top of its screen, otherwise type **www.bing.com/maps** into the **Address** bar of your browser and press the **Enter** key. What displays is shown in Fig. 7.5 overleaf.

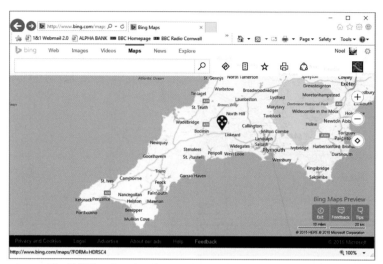

Fig. 7.5 The Opening Screen for my Location on Bing Maps.

Bing Maps puts my location in or near Bodmin, perhaps the nearest location of my Internet Service Provider? When I point to the pin, however, a pop-up tells me to drag the **Pin** icon to the right location. However, this has to be done in stages; first by dragging the **Pin** near one's location, then tapping or clicking on the **Plus** ⊕ button on the map to zoom in, then move the **Pin** nearer the location, and so on. Unfortunately, at some point, the pin just vanished! Even tapping or clicking the **Locate me** ◈ button on the map did not locate the **Pin** again!

Next, I tried to type in my address as the location, but the only recognisable address was that of a commercial enterprise about 300 m away! Nevertheless, I saved this as **My Location** and then tried to obtain directions from it to Redruth. However, the directions given were from Bodmin!

What I can only guess, is that Microsoft took an excellent application (which it was) and is trying to slim it down for tablet users. Perhaps the clue is in the fact that each map is displayed with the stamp '**Bing Maps Preview**' at the bottom right corner. Nevertheless, I then tried to find out what is left of the original program by first asking for directions from my postcode to Redruth (see Fig. 7.6 on the next page).

Fig. 7.6 The Directions Map from my Postcode to Redruth.

At least, the correct route is displayed at last! So far so good, but the postcode covers 5 rural properties spread out in an area of almost one square mile, so for anyone trying to find one of these properties, using **Bing Maps**, will be rather unsuccessful!

Map Views

Depending on your location, there are different map views available in **Bing Maps**. These are controlled by the link at the top of the map area, pointed to in Fig. 7.7.

The **Label** button at the bottom of the screen in Fig. 7.7 becomes active only when the **Aerial**, **Bird's eye** or **Streetside** views are selected. If you tap or click on **Streetside** view and the option is not available for the area, a red 'Peg man' appears on the screen with a minus sign on his chest. In fact it becomes your mouse pointer. The only way of removing it is by pressing the **ESC** key.

Fig. 7.7 Different Views in Bing Maps.

You tap or click the displayed links to change between the available views. In general, they have the following effect:

Road – Displays a traditional style of map with a depiction of roads, borders, rivers, parks and lakes, etc.

Aerial and **Bird's eye** – Displays aerial imagery of the area, both views being the same (perhaps the difference has not been implemented yet). To show road and street names, select **Labels** at the bottom of the screen in Fig. 7.7, but bear in mind that images are not current and their quality depends on the locality.

Streetside – Displays street views, if available for your location.

I suggest you spend some time here to see the effect of all these options, but choose a city for best results.

Searching for a Location

If you want to find details of a particular location you just search for it. You can search for an address, city, town, airport, county, country or continent by typing details in the **Search** box and tapping or clicking the **Search** button. Try searching for **St. Ives**, **Cornwall**. The result is shown in Fig. 7.8.

Fig. 7.8 The Result of a Search for St. Ives in Cornwall.

Bing jumped to the map of the Cornish town, placed a 'marker' on it and included an explanation text in the left pane of the display.

For specific addresses, entering them in the form of **Address, town, post code** usually gives the best results, unless they are not recognised!

In Fig. 7.8, at the bottom of the left pane (you have to scroll down) displays **Points of interest** (photos with links) and a search facility for **Nearby** options. For example, if you type **places to eat** it displays a list of such places with their addresses and telephone numbers, as shown in Fig. 7.9.

Fig. 7.9 The Result of a Search for Places to Eat in St. Ives.

However, some of the listed restaurants are marked on the map with their name, but others are not. Also, included in the St. Ives area are restaurants in Penzance and Gwithian Towans (7.7 and 10 miles away), even though well known restaurants in St. Ives are not included!

Sites with Streetside Views

Before Microsoft tried to shrink **Bing Maps** to presumably accommodate tablet users, it was possible to tap or click a **Streetside** view 🚶 icon, which was to be found at the top of the **Bing Map** area (now replaced by the **Share** option), to change the cursor to a blue 'Peg Man', as shown here, but at the same time displaying a map of blue areas within which a **Streetside** view was available two years ago, as shown for Europe in Fig. 7.10 on the next page.

Fig. 7.10 Available Streetside View Area Coverage.

Now this facility has been removed, and unless you know where **Streetside** view is available in a specific place, the only way of finding out is by trial and error. I hope the above map, even though it is out of date, will prove helpful.

If you try to get **Streetside** view for a specific area and a red 'Peg Man' is displayed, you know this facility is not available to you! So now that we know that the Bristol area is available to us, search for a well known site, such as the **Clifton Suspension Bridge**, to display Fig. 7.11 below.

Fig. 7.11 The Result of a Search in Road View.

If you first try the **Bird's eye** view option, a picture postcard of the bridge displays, as shown below.

Fig. 7.12 The Clifton Suspension Bridge in Bird's Eye View.

In fact, this is a postcard – have a look at the full address in **Bing**'s address box (not shown above) and you'll see that it refers to **upload.wikipedia.org**, that's why it is very difficult to manipulate it, if you tried. To go back, tap or click the left-pointing arrow on the left of the address box to display a series of very interesting pictures of the bridge taken at different times and in different angles, one of which is shown in Fig. 7.13. To see more, tap or click the white arrow head

Fig. 7.13 Selection of Different Views of the Bridge.

Finally, close down the **wikipedia** tab on your browser to return to the **Road** view of the bridge, then select the **Streetside** view and place the cursor, which has changed to a blue 'Peg man', on the bridge to display Fig. 7.14 below.

Fig. 7.14 The Roadside View of the Bridge.

You can follow the road by tapping or clicking on the direction arrows displaying above. Try it.

Navigating the Map Area

With **Bing Maps** you can change what shows in the map viewing area in two dimensions. You can pan the map (move it across the screen at the same scale), and you can zoom in (to see a smaller area in more detail) or out (to see a larger area with less detail). You can navigate around a map using either your finger (on a touch sensitive screen) or the mouse.

Using your finger, you can move around a map by simply touching it and moving in the direction you want to go. To zoom out you just place two fingers on the map and bring them together in a pinch movement and to zoom in you spread your fingers outwards.

Using the mouse can also execute all the necessary operations easily and quickly. For example, to pan the map, just hold the left mouse button down to change the mouse pointer to a hand ⟨🖐⟩ which you use to drag the map around the screen. To zoom in, just roll the mouse wheel away from you, and towards you to zoom out. The zoom will centre on the pointer location on the map.

With these actions (fingers or mouse) you can almost instantly zoom out to view a substantial part of the Earth, as shown in Fig. 7.15 in **Bird's eye** view. You can then move the pointer to a new location and zoom in again to the scale you need.

Fig. 7.15 An Aerial View of Part of the Earth.

To pan the map, you use a finger or point with your mouse and left-click, then drag the map to move it to the direction you want to go.

You can use the two **Navigation** controls to zoom in ⊕ on the centre of the map, and ⊖ to zoom out.

If you prefer using the keyboard, you can zoom in and out with the **+** and **–** keys. You can pan left ⇐, right ⇒, up ⇑, and down ⇓ with the arrow keys. The choice is yours!

Getting Directions

There are several ways in **Bing Maps** to get directions from one location to another. You can type a **from-to** statement into the search field, such as *from St. Ives Cornwall to Oxford*, and tap or click the **Search** button or you can tap or click the **Directions** link and enter a starting and destination location and tap or click the **Go** button.

The first method actually completes the operation as if you had used the second method, as shown in Fig. 7.16 on the next page.

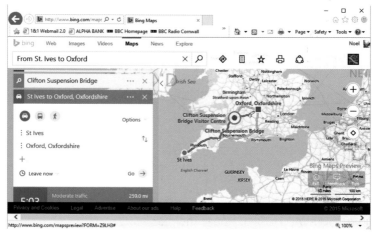

Fig. 7.16 Getting Driving Directions.

The program defaults to giving driving directions and the recommended route appears on the map as a blue line with green and red markers at either end, as shown in Fig. 7.16 above. **Bing Maps** give a total distance, as shown on the left panel of Fig. 7.16 and suggests suitable routes in its detailed, numbered, directions (you might have to scroll down to see these), part of which is shown in Fig. 7.17. You even have a **Print** option.

Fig. 7.17 The Suggested Route.

I leave it to you to investigate other options, such as **Traffic**, **Print** and **Share**. As a map lover I hope when more work has been done on the **Maps** App and **Bing Maps**, a lot of the criticism made will vanish and the end result will be as good as previous versions.

I hope, I have covered enough ground on **Bing Maps** so that you can find your way around them easily.

8

Connectivity & Mobility

Many homes and small offices these days have more than one PC and connecting to a network is a priority so that you can access the Internet from them all, share documents, pictures or music, and print to a single printer. Windows 10 makes this process very much easier than with pre-Windows 7 versions of the Operating System (OS), especially if all the computers are running under the same OS.

Joining a Network

 Although there are many types of networks, such as **Wireless**, **Ethernet**, **HomePNA** and **Powerline**, these days practically everybody uses **Wireless** (WiFi), so only this type of connection is covered here.

To set up a wireless network each computer to be included needs a **Wireless Network Adaptor**, which is built-in these days in all laptops. You will also need a **Wireless Router** to allow access to the Internet and to 'connect' your networked computers.

Your Internet Service Provider (ISP) will often offer an ADSL or combination modem/wireless router as part of your Broadband package and some might even come and install it for you. Others might send you the necessary equipment and a CD to make the installation easier for you.

Once you have obtained and installed all this hardware (if not installed already) you could, if you so wish, run the **Set up a new network** wizard from the main PC that is attached to the router.

To start the process of networking, touch and hold or right-click the **Start** button and select **Network and Sharing** entry from the displayed **Control Panel** options when in **Large icons** view, as shown in Fig. 8.1 below.

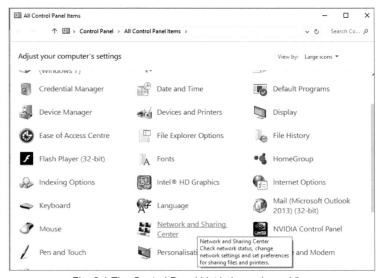

Fig. 8.1 The Control Panel List in Large Icons View.

Selecting the **Network and Sharing** option in Fig. 8.1, opens Fig. 8.2 displaying basic network and set up options.

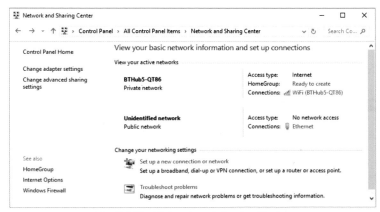

Fig. 8.2 The Network and Sharing Center.

Microsoft has not bothered to change the spelling of **Center** in **Control Panel** when viewed in large icons! Nevertheless, as you can see in Fig. 8.2, the **Network and Sharing Center** has identified my WiFi connection which is a BT Hub5 router.

However, to set up a new connection you tap or click the **Set up a connection or network** option which displays Fig. 8.3 below.

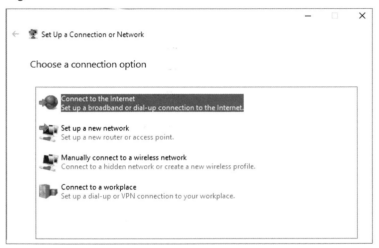

Fig. 8.3 The Set up a New Connection or Network Option.

To continue, tap or click the **Set up a new network** option (if not yet connected). You will be stepped through the process of adding other computers and devices to the network.

Network Connection

With Windows 10 if a computer has a working network adaptor, the **Network** icon appears in the **System Tray** area at the right end of the **Taskbar**. This icon indicates whether your network adaptor is an **Ethernet** 🖳 adaptor or a wireless 🛜 adaptor with more circular segments indicating stronger signal. When the computer is not connected to a network, a yellow exclamation shows on the connection 🖳 icon, while when a wireless connection is not available, the icon is dimmer with an asterisk 🛜 added to it.

When you physically connect your computer to a network with an **Ethernet** cable, Windows automatically creates the network connection, but to connect to a wireless network for

Fig. 8.4 Connecting to a Network.

the first time, you might need to select your Broadband connection and make the connection yourself by tapping or clicking the **Connect automatically** box to select it, then tapping or clicking the **Connect** button in Fig. 8.4. If a **WPA** password is required, you will be prompted to enter it, and then Windows will connect to the selected network.

Wireless Network Security

For very obvious reasons, when you set up a wireless network you should set it up so that only people you choose can access it. There are several wireless network security systems available, but the most common these days is:

WPA   (Wi-Fi Protected Access) encrypts information, checks to make sure that the network security key has not been modified and also authenticates users to help ensure that only authorised people can access the network.

Also 802.1x authentication can help enhance security for 802.11 type wireless networks and wired **Ethernet** networks. It can work with the **WPA** key and uses an authentication server to validate users and provide network access. This is used mainly in company networks.

HomeGroup

The easiest way of getting to **HomeGroup** is via the **Control Panel** shown in Fig. 8.1 on page 130 or from the **Network and Sharing Center** (if it is still open on your screen) shown in Fig. 8.2 also on page 130. This feature simplifies the whole network procedure, particularly when the networked PCs are running under Windows 10, but not necessarily so.

Tapping or clicking the **HomeGroup** icon, opens the screen shown in Fig. 8.5 with the option to **Create a homegroup** at the bottom of the screen.

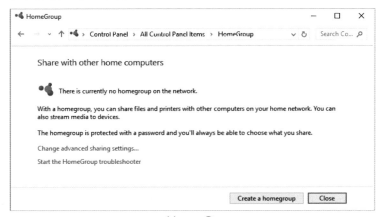

Fig. 8.5 The HomeGroup Screen.

Tapping or clicking this button, starts the process. On a subsequent screen (not shown here), you are informed that you can share files and printers with other computers and that you can stream media to devices. Tapping or clicking the **Next** button on this screen, displays Fig. 8.6 in which you can choose what else you want to share.

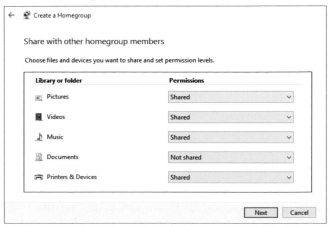

Fig. 8.6 Changing HomeGroup Permissions.

Now select what you want to share from a list of your default folders (**Pictures**, **Videos**, **Music** and **Documents**) and your printers. Having done so, tap or click on **Next** to display a screen similar to that in Fig. 8.7.

Fig. 8.7 The Password Required to Join PCs to the HomeGroup.

You have to use this password to add all your other computers on your home network to the **HomeGroup**. Quite a tedious operation, but it doesn't take long and in the end is well worth the trouble.

When I first connected my Windows 7 PC to the **HomeGroup**, I was asked to provide the user name and password of my Windows 10 PC on which I had set up the **HomeGroup** – these are what you use to log on to the latter.

> **Note:** It is important to restart the computers for these changes to take effect.

All your Windows computers in the same **HomeGroup** can share folders, files, devices and media without ever having to type passwords whenever anything is accessed. You select what you want shared on each computer and as long as it is 'awake' it can be accessed from the other computers in the group with just a few taps or clicks. You can even change what is shared, as shown in Fig. 8.6 on the previous page.

Accessing HomeGroup Computers

Once the **HomeGroup** is created and all your home computers are joined, accessing their shared folders is very easy. Just open up **File Explorer** and tap or click on **Network** in the **Navigation** pane. In Fig. 8.8, you see the computers that are turned on and are not in sleep mode.

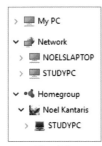

Fig. 8.8.

The STUDYPC is the computer I am on right now (running Windows 10), while NOELSLAPTOP is a computer on the network (running Windows 7) and I can access all its folders. Tapping or clicking on a folder will open up all the folders and files in it. Very quick and easy.

> **Note:** Tapping or clicking on **Homegroup** only shows the contents of the computer you are currently using. To see all the computers currently awake, tap or click on **Network**.

Sharing Printers

To share printers on your network, even if they are not in a **HomeGroup**, so everyone in your household can connect as long as the printers and PCs are switched on, you do as follows:

On the computer that the printer is attached to, navigate to the **Control Panel**, then tap or click the **Devices and Printers** link shown in Fig. 8.9.

Fig. 8.9 The Devices and Printers Link in Control Panel.

On the opened **Devices and Printers** window, locate the printer attached to the computer, touch and hold or right-click and select **Set as default printer** from the displayed drop-down menu, if not already selected.

For the same printer, touch and hold or right-click and

select **Printer properties** from the displayed drop-down menu, shown in Fig. 8.10 to open the **Properties** dialogue box, then tap or click the **Sharing** tab, and tap or click the [⚙ Change Sharing Options] button. Next, tap or click the **Share this printer** box to select it, then press **OK** to approve the options and close the **Properties** dialogue box (Fig. 8.11).

Fig. 8.10.

Before you can use a shared printer from your other computers on the network, you have to add it to the list of available printers on each of the PCs by opening the **Devices and Printers** window and selecting the [Add a printer] button and choosing your printer from the list that displays. Wait for the printer driver to be located and loaded. Now any computer on the

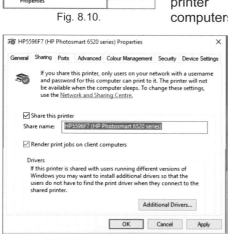

Fig. 8.11 Sharing a Printer.

network can select the printer and use it just as if it were directly connected to it, but it requires the PC which is connected to the printer to be on.

Note: A wireless printer is detected by all the PCs on the network, which greatly simplifies sharing a printer.

Mobility

By mobility I am referring here to computer mobility, not your ability to get around! One of the nice things about using Windows 10 on a **mobile** notebook or netbook PC is that the most important configuration options are consolidated into a single utility, the **Windows Mobility Center**. This is where you should go when you want to control how your mobile PC works.

Windows Mobility Center

To launch the **Mobility Center**, touch and hold or right-click the **Start** button, then select the **Control Panel** option from the displayed menu. As I mentioned earlier, Microsoft did not change the spelling of **Center** in **Control Panel** when viewed in large icons!

Anyway, at nearly the very end of the **Control Panel** list,

Fig. 8.12.

you will find the **Windows Mobility Center** link shown here in Fig. 8.12. Tapping or clicking on this link, opens a window like the one in Fig. 8.13 below.

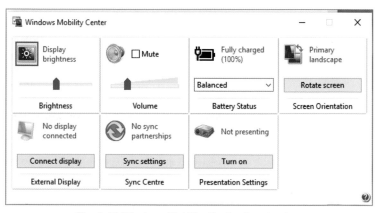

Fig. 8.13 Windows Mobility Center for a Laptop.

The **Mobility Center** includes panels for the most common laptop settings. These are:

Brightness

 Display brightness

A slider temporarily adjusts the display brightness. If you hover the mouse over the display icon it turns into a button which opens the **Power Options** window, where you can change the brightness level on your current power plan.

Volume

 ☐ Mute

Adjusts the volume level of your computer's sound and lets you mute it. Tap or click the speaker graphic to open the **Sound** dialogue box where you can adjust all the audio settings on your laptop.

Battery Status

 Fully charged (100%)

Displays the current charge status of your computer's battery and lets you change the power plan. Tap or click the battery graphic, to open the **Power Options** window where you can edit the power plans and create your own custom power plans, as discussed in the next section.

Screen Orientation

 Primary landscape

Displays the orientation of your screen. Tap or click the screen graphic to open the **Screen Resolution** panel, where you can change the appearance of your display.

External Display

 No display connected

Lets you connect your laptop to an external monitor or projector. Tap or click the display graphic to open the **Screen Resolution** window where you can change the resolution and orientation of both your internal and external displays.

Tap or click the **Connect display** button to open the options available for projecting to a secondary screen.

Sync Center

No sync partnerships

Lets you check the results of your recent synchronisation activity if you've set up your computer to sync files with a network server.

All in all, this is a very useful facility for mobile users. Some notebook manufacturers might include their own panels.

> **Note:** The **Mobility Center** by default, is only available on laptops, netbooks, and tablets. It is not available on desktop computers unless it is enabled.

Power & Sleep Settings

If you are worried when using a laptop away from the mains about how much power it is using, then read on as even the best batteries seem to run low far too quickly!

As well as the **Battery Status** tile in the **Mobility Center**, the battery meter in the **System Tray** area of the **Taskbar** shows you the state of your laptop's battery. If you tap it or click it, a pop-up like that in Fig. 8.14 opens showing what power plan is active

Fig. 8.14 Battery Status.

(**Battery saver** in this case and a **Display brightness** at 30%).

Windows 10 caters for different power settings that can help you save energy. To see these plans, tap or click the **Power & sleep settings** link in the pop-up of Fig. 8.14 to open the screen in Fig. 8.15 on the next page.

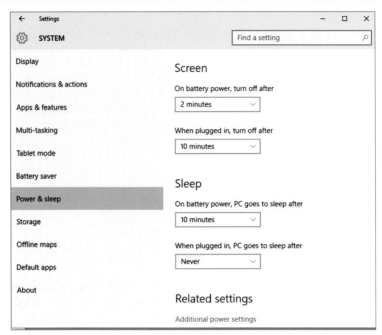

Fig. 8.15 The Power Options Window.

On this screen you can set the maximum time for switching off the screen and/or putting your laptop to sleep when on battery and/or when plugged into a power socket.

There is an additional setting that you can visit by tapping or clicking the **Battery saver** option in the left pane of the above screen to get information on the estimated time remaining on the battery and activate the battery saver option. Do have a look!

Finally you can open the **Power Options** window by tapping or clicking the **Additional power settings** link at the bottom of Fig. 8.15, to open the display in Fig. 8.16, shown on the next page.

On that screen you can choose two power options; **Balanced** or **Power saver** and you can also specify various control options, such what to do when the power button is pressed, or the lid of the laptop is closed.

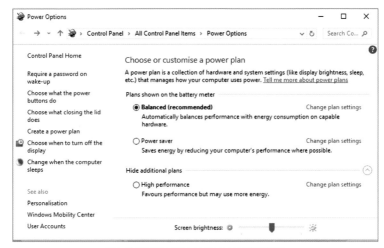

Fig. 8.16 The Power Options Window.

In the above screen, I have also chosen to **Show additional plans**, which by default are hidden, namely the **High performance** plan.

The three default **Power Plans** are:

Balanced – Giving good performance when it is needed, but saving power during periods of inactivity.

Power saver – Saves power by reducing screen brightness and system performance. This can be useful if you are ever 'caught out'.

High performance – Giving maximum brightness and performance, but using far more power, making it rather unhelpful to mobile users unless they are plugged in to the mains.

Which plan to use? For most people much of the time the default **Balanced** plan is a good compromise between battery life and performance. Many people will never change from this recommended option.

When you are away from home and operating on batteries the **Power saver** plan will probably give you a few more minutes of battery life, but do remember to reduce display brightness as this uses more power than any other part of a computer. Also disconnect devices that you are not actually using, such as USB devices which use power just by being connected.

You should only really use the **High performance** plan when you are connected to mains power and have a full battery charge.

These three power plans should meet your needs most of the time, but if you want to build your own, then you can use one of the default power plans as a starting point. All of them can be adapted by clicking on their **Change plan settings** link in the **Power Options** window.

You do have lots of option to examine and think about their effect, so spending some time here might be worthwhile.

9

Some Useful Apps

There are several Apps to be found in the **All apps** list, worth looking at, such as **Alarms & Clocks**, **Calculator**, **Health & Fitness**, **Money**, **News**, etc. Some of the most important of these Apps are covered here (in alphabetical order), but not those that are about to be withdrawn in the next month or so.

Alarms & Clocks

The screen below shows this App with the **World Clock** option selected. The other options are for setting an **Alarm**, a **Timer** and **Stopwatch**.

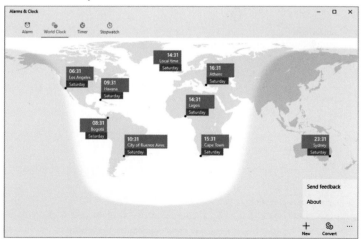

Fig. 9.1 Times at Different Parts of the World.

Selecting the three dots at the bottom right corner of the above screen, opens the menu shown. Use the + button to display a box in which you type the name of a city to get the time at that location. However, you can only add 10 cities on the map!

Calculator

As you can see from the composite below, the **Calculator** has many functions, but most people might be more interested in the **Converter** part of it. Tapping or clicking the **Menu** ≡ button at the top left corner of the screen, displays several options.

In Fig. 9.2 below, the **Volume** option was selected and a composite of all the menu options and the result of choosing one such option is presented. In your case, the menu options will obscure the area of selection of types of volume.

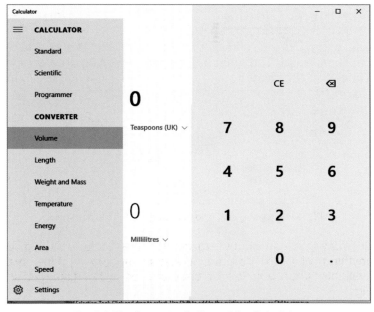

Fig. 9.2 The Converter Options of the Calculator.

You can convert Teaspoons (UK) to Millilitres; Inches to Centimetres; Kilograms to Pounds; Fahrenheit to Celsius; Joules to Food calories; Square feet to Square metres; Kilometres per hour to Miles per hour.

Within each selected conversion screen, there are additional options you can choose from. For example, select **Volume** to display the screen in Fig. 9.2 shown on the previous page, then tap or click the first conversion option, in this case **Teaspoons (UK)**, displays more options as shown in Fig. 9.3 below.

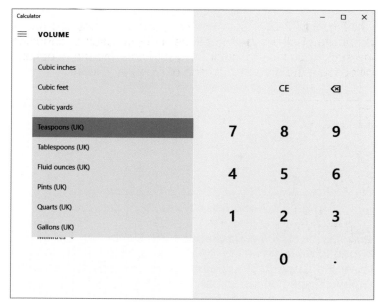

Fig. 9.3 Choosing an Options to Convert from in Volume.

So, now you can choose to convert practically anything to anything else in **Volume**, because related options are available when you tap or click one of those displayed in Fig. 9.3.

However, this process is reversible. For example, referring to Fig. 9.2, on the previous page, the default conversion option is 'from top to bottom' because the **0** above **Teaspoons (UK)** is emboldened. To reverse the process and force the conversion to become 'from bottom to top', simply tap or click the bottom **0** (the one above **Millilitres**) to embolden it. On the next page, I demonstrate this process.

Referring to Fig. 9.2 on page 144, select **Fluid ounces (UK)** from the menu of options when the arrowhead ⌄ against the **Teaspoons (UK)** is tapped or clicked. Then, tap or click the arrowhead ⌄ against the **Millilitres** and select **Cups (US)**. Now, selecting 8 from the numeric keypad on the screen, displays Fig. 9.4 below.

Fig. 9.4 Converting Fluid Ounces (UK) to Cups (US).

Next, tap or click the **Backspace** ⌫ symbol on the screen keypad to clear the entries back to zero, then tap the actual 0 above the **Cups (US)** to embolden it, then select 1 from the numeric keypad on the screen, to display Fig. 9.5.

Fig. 9.5 Converting Cups (US) to Fluid Ounces (UK).

Health & Fitness

 A composite of the opening screen of the **Health & Fitness** App in displayed in Fig. 9.6 below. In your case, to see the whole of the **Quick Access** menu, you'll need to swipe to the left, but that will obscure part of the young man in the photo.

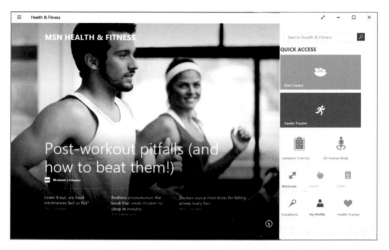

Fig. 9.6 The Health & Fitness Composite Opening Screen.

As you can see, there is a lot of information to look at here. You could start by looking at the **Diet Tracker**, then **Cardio Tracker**, before looking at the **Workouts**, **Health Tracker** and **Exercises**. I already feel the benefits!

However, before you can do anything in this rather unfriendly App, you need to fill in your **Profile**, as shown in Fig. 9.7.

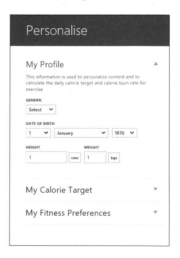

Fig. 9.7 Your Profile.

Money

If you have a financial or business interest in company stocks and shares, mutual funds and international currency rates, then the **Money** App will be useful to you. If not, you can probably skip the rest of this section. Windows 10's **Money** offers an easy way to search for share prices, mutual fund details and financial information on publicly listed companies.

To access the **Money** page, simply tap or click the **Money** tile on the **Start** screen to open the first screen with the most recent news on finance, as shown in Fig. 9.8

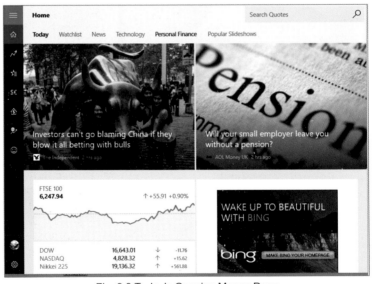

Fig. 9.8 Today's Opening Money Page.

The opening page should look similar to the one above, but obviously with different content. To the left of the page are menu options **Markets**, **Watchlist**, **Currencies**, **Mortgage Calculator** and **World Markets** with additional options at the top of the screen.

If you have obtained any quotes, these will be listed under **Watchlist**, as shown in Fig. 9.9 on the next page.

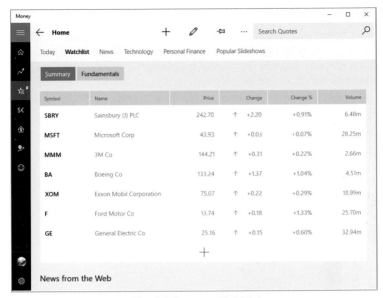

Fig. 9.9 Items on Watchlist.

To search for 'Quotes' of mutual funds or stock market companies, start typing in the **Search** box at the top of screen. As you type in the first part of a name a list instantly appears with suggestions on what you might be looking for, as shown in Fig. 9.10 below. You just tap or click the option you want in the list, say SBRY, the ticker symbol is automatically placed in the **Watchlist**, and the screen changes to a detailed page of data on the Company, as shown in Fig. 9.11 on the next page.

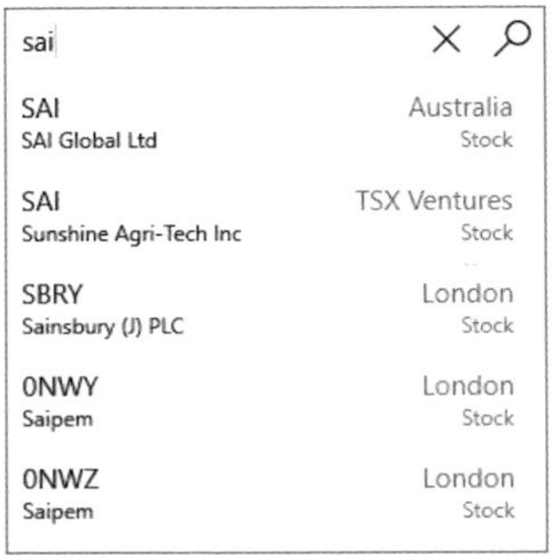

The contents of the above screen tend to be time-dependant, so you might see a different list for the same search criteria.

Fig. 9.10 The Autosuggestion List.

Company Summary

This gives an overview of the current financial situation of the selected UK company, with access to its performance by **Day**, **Week**, **Month** etc., which you can choose from a list at the bottom of the screen of Fig. 9.11.

Fig. 9.11 SBRY Day Performance Chart.

Swiping to the left reveals screens which include summaries on **Key Statistics**, **Fund Growth**, **Profitability**, etc., one of which is shown in Fig. 9.12 below. Swiping upwards displays news on the Company.

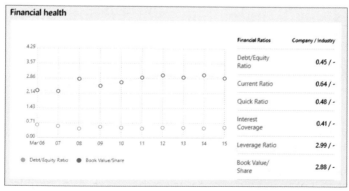

Fig. 9.12 Performance of Related Companies.

There is a lot more to this App, but I leave it to you to explore.

News

 These days every newspaper, TV news station and other sources of information have Web sites showing a continuously updated online version of their news and story contents. We all like to know what is happening, where and when.

Windows 10 shows live content of news continuously as it happens, as shown in Fig. 9.13 below.

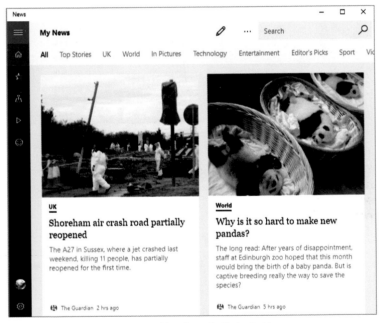

Fig. 9.13 The Top Story in Today's News.

By the time you are reading this, the news would have changed, so a different picture will be displayed.

Although it is possible to use **bing** to search for news, it is not as satisfying visually as using the **News** App, so it is not worth spending time on the search engine.

News Layout

You can swipe to the left or tap or click the heading at the top of the screen to see more sections under headings like **Top Stories**, **UK**, **World**, **In Pictures**, **Technology**, etc. In other words, everything to keep you occupied for quite a long time!

Each section has several topics within it, as shown in Fig. 9.14.

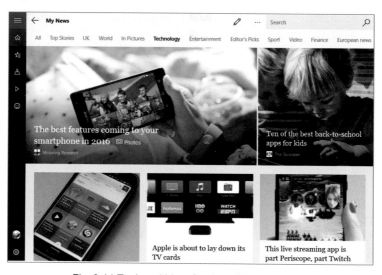

Fig. 9.14 Topics within a Section of Today's News.

Look on your screen to see when the last update was made which shows that you do get up-to-date news. When the mouse pointer passes over a topic, it highlights it indicating that if you tap or click, the full story of that topic will display.

Once a topic is selected, large arrowheads display in the middle of the screen, as shown in Fig. 9.15, which can be used to go to the next or previous article.

Fig. 9.15 Navigation Arrowheads.

Phone Companion

Selecting the **Phone Companion** All from the **All apps** of the **Start** menu, displays the screen shown in Fig. 9.16 below.

Fig. 9.16 The Opening Screen of Phone Companion.

Depending on which type of phone you have, select the appropriate image from this screen above to open a window similar to the one shown in Fig. 9.17 below for the iPhone.

Fig. 9.17 The Get Started Screen of Phone Companion.

As you can see from the available **Get Started** screen options, at present you can select to:

- Automatically get the photos you take with your iPhone or iPad onto your PC.

- Synchronise anything you enter into OneNote with your iPhone.

- Use Skype on your iPhone or iPad which is free to make video calls and send messages over WiFi.

- Use Word, Excel and PowerPoint on your iPhone or iPad and everything you do on your iPhone or iPad using these Apps is automatically updated on your PC.

- Get you e-mail messages and calendar with Outlook on your iPhone or iPad. However, Outlook is different from Office Outlook – just to let you know!

Of these options, I'll test **Word**'s capability to see how it behaves. I first connected my iPad to my Windows 10 PC and selected **Word** from the list shown in Fig. 9.18.

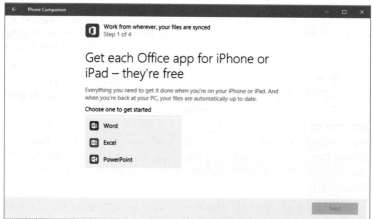

Fig. 9.18 Getting Office Apps for the iPad.

Selecting **Word**, and tapping or clicking **Next**, displays a screen where a choice has to be made between **iPhone** or **iPad**. I select the iPad and provided my e-mail address.

Next, tapping or clicking the **Send** button to submit the request, an e-mail was prepared for me and I was asked to approve it and send it, with a reminder to open the e-mail on the iPad and follow the links provided from there. The e-mail was never received!

However, another option also available was to download Microsoft **Word** from the **App Store** (or **iTunes**), shown in Fig. 9.19.

I downloaded Word, Excel and PowerPoint in turn and after the first download, I was asked to sign in, *but* with the e-mail and password used on my Windows 10 PC. This is very important. Maybe thats why I did not receive the e-mail?

Next, returning to the Windows 10 PC and continuing, I was asked to verify that I had signed in, after which the final screen was displayed asking me to upgrade to the full Office 365 version. This, of

Fig. 9.19 Downloading Office Apps for the iPad from App Store.

course, costs money every time it is used, so I chose to stay with the light version. Tapping or clicking the **Done** button, returns to the screen of Fig. 9.17 (page 153), from which one can either repeat the process with the other two Apps or close the window. Subsequent downloads do not require to be signed in, as credentials are recognised from the first download.

On starting one of the three Apps, say **Word**, a menu appears on the left of the opening screen with options to create a **New** document, open **Recent** documents or just **Open** an existing document, as shown in Fig. 9.20 on the next page. The same menu options appear on **Excel** and **PowerPoint**.

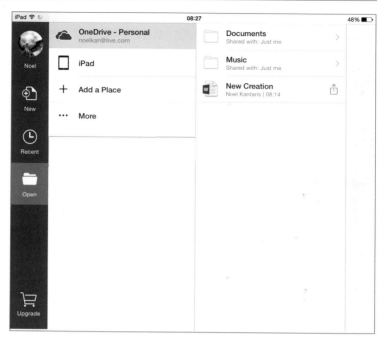

Fig. 9.20 The Opening Screen for Word on the iPad.

When you select to **Open** an existing document you are offered places where your documents might be found, such a **OneDrive**, provided you have documents saved there. You are also given the option to add other **Cloud** locations or get documents from the iPad itself.

I have tested these three Apps and they all work fine. For example, I opened an existing document on **OneDrive**, using the iPad, added to it extra lines, then opened it on the Windows 10 PC and found the additions there. I then deleted part of the document on the PC and returning to the iPad found that the changes were carried through.

A very worthwhile addition to your iPad or iPhone, but with limited functionality. If that is not good enough for you, there is always the option to subscribe to the cloud version of Office!

Weather

These days the weather is an integral part of news and finance. It certainly has a profound effect on both of these, so I decided to include it in this chapter.

Tapping or clicking the **Weather** App displays the following screen.

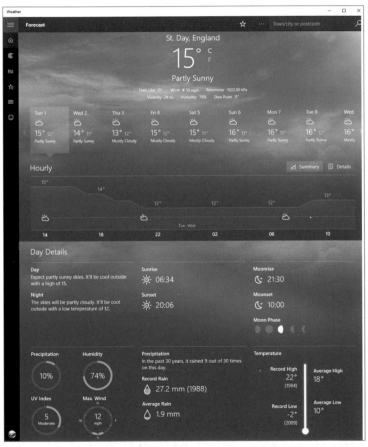

Fig. 9.21 The Weather at a Locality.

The screen in Fig. 9.21 is a composite. To see the bottom half of it, you'll have to swipe upwards or with the mouse use the scroll bar.

The **Weather** App allows you to customise it and include other localities, but to begin with it senses where you are, so what is displayed when you first start is related to your area.

The menu options to the left of the screen, provide the following functionality:

Menu Option	*Function*
Forecast	Displays today's weather and a forecast for an additional 8 days, using **Summary** view which can be changed to **Details** view.
Maps	Fills the screen with a detailed map of a large area (several square miles) with your location pinpointed in the middle. At the bottom of the screen, a video type facility can show the changes in temperature for the next 24 hours on the actual full map.
Historical Weather	Displays a bar type chart for each month from January to December with statistics on temperature and rainfall.
Places	Displays your location and any other favourite places you chose to add. This allows you to see the forecast for different locations.
News	Displays several pages of weather news around the world with photos and some interesting videos, but the inevitable advert spoils the enjoyment!

There is more to this App than first meets the eye, so have a look and enjoy it!

10

Accessibility

The Ease of Access Centre

If you have problems using a standard computer Windows 10 has several features that may be of help.

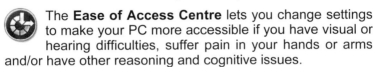 The **Ease of Access Centre** lets you change settings to make your PC more accessible if you have visual or hearing difficulties, suffer pain in your hands or arms and/or have other reasoning and cognitive issues.

You can open the **Ease of Access Centre** by touching and holding or right-clicking the **Start** button, then selecting **Control Panel** and tapping or clicking the **Ease of Access Centre**, as shown in Fig. 10.1.

Fig. 10.1 The Ease of Access Centre Entry in the Control Panel.

Tapping or clicking the option in Fig. 10.1, opens the screen shown in Fig. 10.2 on the next page.

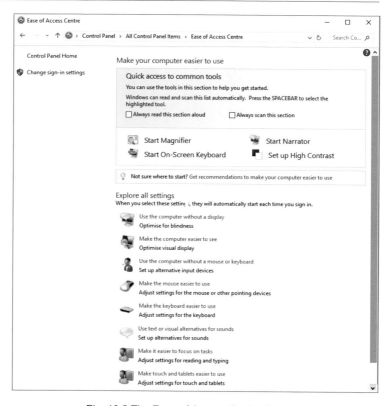

Fig. 10.2 The Ease of Access Centre Screen.

The **Ease of Access Centre** includes a quick access panel at the top with a highlight rotating through the four most common tools; **Start Magnifier**, **Start Narrator**, **Start On-Screen Keyboard**, and **Set up High Contrast**. A voice, the Narrator, also tells you what option is selected.

If the Narrator annoys you, tap or click the **Always read this section aloud** box to remove the tick mark from it. While you are doing this, you could also remove the tick mark from the **Always scan this section** box, to stop the focus from rotating between the four entries.

The ☼ **Get recommendations to make your computer easier to use** link opens a five-stage questionnaire.

Depending on your answers to questions about performing routine tasks, such as whether you have difficulty seeing faces or text on TV, hearing conversations, or using a pen or pencil, Windows will provide a recommendation of the accessibility settings and programs that are likely to improve your ability to see, hear and use your computer. This has to be a good place to start.

The **Explore all settings** section below the **Get recommendations ...** link in the **Ease of Access Centre** lets you explore settings options by categories. When selected, these will automatically start each time you log on to the computer. They include:

- Using the computer without a display

- Making the computer easier to see

- Using the computer without a mouse or keyboard

- Making a mouse easier to use

- Making the keyboard easier to use

- Using text or visual alternatives for sounds

- Making it easier to focus on tasks

- Making touch and tablets easier to use.

In the next few pages I will give you an overview of these various options, but I will not discuss any of them in too much detail, as different people have different and specific needs!

The Magnifier

To start the **Magnifier**, click on **Start Magnifier** (words not icon) shown in Fig. 10.3.

Fig. 10.3 Computer Screen with the Magnifier Active.

The new **Magnifier** window has two views: **Full screen** (the default), and **Lens,** selected from the **Views** drop-down list shown open in the composite screen dump in Fig. 10.3. To rotate through these views, use the key combinations:

For Full screen view   **Ctrl+Alt+F**
For Lens view   **Ctrl+Alt+L**
For Docked view   **Ctrl+Alt+D**

This is important because what is supposed to happen in **Lens** view (which is that wherever you place the mouse pointer the screen is magnified), does not work (it used to on previous Windows versions) and should you try it, the only way of exiting from it is to use the **Full** view shortcut as detailed above.

In **Full** view, the **Magnifier** window allows you to increase ⊕ or decrease ⊖ the magnification, or use the **Options** icon ⚙ to turn on colour inversion, select tracking options and fine-tune screen fonts.

If you don't use the **Magnifier** window for more than a few seconds, it turns into an actual magnifying glass icon, as shown here. Clicking this **Magnifier** icon again, reopens the **Magnifier** window shown in Fig. 10.3 on the previous page.

To close down the **Magnifier,** click the **Close** ⊠ button in the **Magnifier** window.

The Narrator

Narrator is a basic screen reader built into Windows and may be useful for the visually impaired. It reads dialogue boxes and window controls in a number of Windows basic applications.

To open the **Narrator,** tap or click the **Start Narrator** option in the **Ease of Access Centre** (Fig. 10.2, page 160). Another way to start **Narrator** is to use the key combination ⊞**+Enter. Narrator** will start speaking in a rather hard to understand electronic voice reading everything that you point at with your finger or the mouse.

After starting **Narrator**, an icon is placed on the **Taskbar**. Tapping or clicking that icon opens the **Narrator Settings** screen in which you can:

- Change how **Narrator** starts

- Change how you interact with your PC

- Change the pitch or volume of the current voice or choose an alternative voice.

Finally, it might be worth visiting the **Narrator** keyboard commands screen to find out what commands are available to control **Narrator**. You do this by using the key combination **CapsLock+F1**. On the screen that opens, you'll find both keyboard commands and touch commands to completely control **Narrator**. While you are looking at these commands, you can stop **Narrator** from going on reading one command after another, by pressing the **Ctrl** key.

If you find this **Narrator** useful you will need to play around with it for a while until you get familiar with the way it works.

Note: To close **Narrator** just use the key combination **CapsLock+Esc**. **Narrator** even tells you that it is about to exit!

The On-Screen Keyboard

To activate the **On-Screen Keyboard** (Fig. 10.4), click the **Start**, **On-Screen Keyboard** option in the **Ease of Access Centre** shown earlier in Fig. 10.2 on page 160.

Fig. 10.4 The On-screen Keyboard.

This excellent virtual keyboard opens on the screen and allows users with mobility impairments to type data using a mouse pointer, a joystick, or other pointing device. The result is exactly as if you were using the actual keyboard. It has three typing modes selected when the **Options** key on the virtual keyboard is tapped or clicked.

The three modes of the virtual keyboard are:

Click on keys mode – you tap or click the on-screen keys to type text (the default mode).

Hover over keys mode – you use a finger, a mouse or joystick to point to a key for a predefined period of time, and the selected character is typed automatically.

Scan through keys mode – the **On-screen Keyboard** continually scans the keyboard and highlights areas where you can type keyboard characters by pressing a hot key or using a switch-input device.

You can also adjust the settings for your 'physical' keyboard by clicking the **Make the keyboard easier to use** entry towards the middle of the **Ease of Access Centre** window (see Fig. 10.2, page 160) and selecting various options on the displayed window.

On the 'Make the keyboard easier to use' screen you can:

Turn on Mouse Keys – lets you move the mouse pointer by pressing the arrow keys on the keyboard's numeric pad.

Turn on Sticky Keys – allows you to press the **Ctrl**, **Alt**, and **Shift**, keys one at a time, instead of all at the same time. This is useful for people who have difficulty pressing two or more keys at a time.

Turn on Toggle Keys – makes your computer play a high-pitched sound when the **Caps Lock**, **Scroll Lock**, or **Num Lock** keys are used. The **Turn on Filter Keys** option tells the keyboard to ignore brief or repeated keystrokes.

The Display Options

To make your screen easier to see you can try the **Set up High Contrast** option in Fig. 10.2, page 160 . This opens yet another window, as shown in Fig. 10.5, in which you can set programs to change their colour-specific schemes to a **High Contrast** scheme, change the size of text, set the thickness of the blinking cursor, etc.

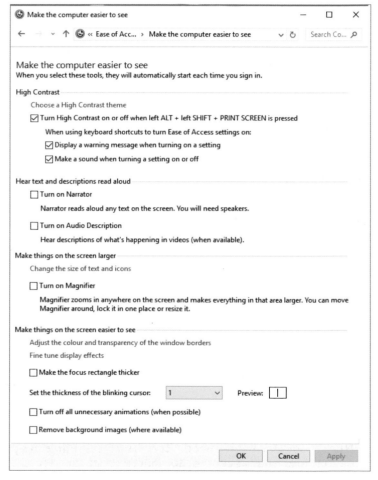

Fig. 10.5 The Make the Computer Easier to See Screen.

The Mouse Options

Clicking the **Make the mouse easier to use** 🖝 link near the middle of Fig. 10.2 (page 160), displays the window below.

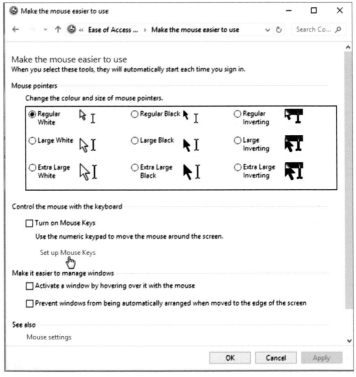

Fig. 10.6 Making the Mouse Easier to Use.

In the above screen you can change the colour and size of the mouse pointer, and control its movements with the keys on the numeric keypad.

Tapping or clicking the **Set up Mouse Keys** link, pointed to in Fig. 10.6, displays an additional window in which you can control, amongst other things, the speed at which the mouse pointer moves, and the shortcut key combination you need to activate and deactivate the numeric keypad.

I'll leave it to you to explore the other settings on the list in the lower half of the **Ease of Access Center**.

11

Looking After Your PC

Windows 10 comes equipped with a full range of utilities for you to easily maintain your PC's health and well being. You can access some of these tools by touching and holding or right-clicking the **Start** button to display the menu shown in Fig. 11.1.

Next, select the **System** option to display the **System** information screen shown in Fig. 11.2 below.

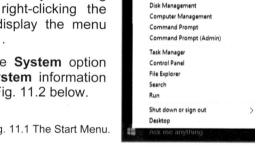

Fig. 11.1 The Start Menu.

Fig. 11.2 The System Information Screen.

This is the easiest way to take a first look at your PC's information – it displays such things as the Operating System, System Summary, Hardware Resources, etc. However, each computer is bound to be different, so don't expect to see the same information. What is important here are the links at the left of the screen which deal with prevention of problems.

Problem Prevention

Windows has strong protection against **System** corruption:

- System Protection
- System Restore
- Automatic Update

Each of these will be discussed separately.

System Protection

Windows applications sometimes can, and do, overwrite important **System** files. Windows protects your **System** files by automatically saving them at regular intervals, but you must check the settings and if necessary change them.

The first setting to be checked is the **System Protection**. To do this, tap or click the **System protection** link at the top-left corner in Fig. 11.2 to open the tabbed dialogue box shown in Fig. 11.3.

With the **System Protection** tab selected, check that the C: drive (the one that Windows is installed on), under **Protection Settings** in Fig. 11.3, is **On**.

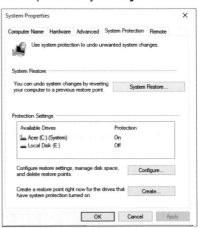

Fig. 11.3 System Protection Tab.

If not, select the option, then tap or click the **Configure** button and tap or click the **Turn on system protection** radio button on the displayed screen to select it. Next, move the slider next to **Max Usage** to, say, 2% to indicate the maximum disc space to be used for system protection. Selecting **OK**, returns you to the dialogue box of Fig. 11.3 where you should tap or click the **Create** button to create a restore point right now. On the dialogue box that opens, give the restore point a descriptive name, and tap or click **Create**.

In the future, you can undo system changes by reverting your PC to the state it was when you created the restore point. This is done by activating the **System Restore** button in Fig. 11.3 which starts the **System Restore** Wizard. Tapping or clicking **Next** displays a dialogue box with all your **Restore** points for you to choose from. **Restore** points are created automatically by the system every time you install or uninstall a program.

Automatic Update

Windows can automatically update any **System** files as they become available from Microsoft's Web site. To make sure this happens, tap or click the **Start** button and select **Settings** to display the screen in Fig. 11.4 below.

Fig. 11.4 The Settings Options Screen.

From these **Settings** select the **Update & security** option, shown here, to display Fig. 11.5 (see next page). Of the options offered, I shall only touch on the first three.

Fig. 11.5 The Windows Update Option Screen.

The system is normally set to automatically install updates. You can check by using the **Advanced options** button. This is important as it guarantees that you are always up to date with security issues that are found and corrected by Microsoft.

Windows Defender

Windows Defender is free anti-spyware and anti-virus software that comes with Windows. It helps protect your computer against spyware and other potentially dangerous software being installed on your computer when you are connected to the Internet.

Tapping or clicking the **Windows Defender** option in Fig. 11.5, displays the **Real-time protection** option screen and a **Cloud-based Protection** option. If you don't have any other Internet security software, it is worth having a look at these. At the very end of the displayed screen, you can select the **Use Windows Defender** link to activate its protection.

Windows Defender offers two ways to help keep infections at bay:

- In real-time, it alerts you when spyware attempts to install itself on your computer, tries to run on it, or attempts to change Windows settings.

- At any time, you can scan for spyware that might be installed on your computer, having bypassed Windows **Defender**, and automatically remove them and the problems they may cause.

If you decide to use **Windows Defender**, then you need to also activate the **Windows Firewall**.

Windows Firewall

For your PC to be secure, make sure that the **Windows Firewall** is switched on. To do so, go to the **Control Panel** and tap or click the **Windows Firewall** link shown here.

A **Firewall** is a software security system that sits between your computer and the outside world and is used to set restrictions on what information is passed to and from the Internet. In other words it protects you from uninvited access.

If your **Firewall** is turned off, or you do not have up-to-date virus protection, the **Action Centre** on the **System Tray** of the **Taskbar** will let you know via the **Notifications** icon.

Backing Up Your Data

Anyone can lose files by either accidentally deleting or replacing them, a virus attack, or a software or hardware failure, such as a complete hard disc failure. With Windows, you can use **System Restore** to recover your system files, you can reinstall your programs, but not your precious data files or pictures and videos of your family.

To protect these, Windows 10 provides automatic regular backups using the **File History** feature. It backs up your files to another internal or external drive and you can restore them if the originals are lost, damaged or deleted. You can configure what you want to back up on a screen that displays when you choose the **Backup** option in Fig. 11.5 shown on the previous page.

If, however, you need to make an 'image backup' of your whole drive, meaning everything on your hard drive, Windows **System** files, all your additional installed programs and all your data, then you have to resort to programs specifically design for the purpose. A quick search on the Internet should reveal a host of such programs, but make quite sure that the one you choose is compatible with Windows 10 (many might not be)!

Hard Disc Management

There are two ways in Windows 10 to help you keep your hard disc in good condition: **Disk Clean-up**, which removes unnecessary files from your hard disc and frees up space, and **Optimise and defragment drive** which optimises your hard discs by rearranging their data to eliminate unused spaces, which speeds up access to your hard discs.

Disc Clean-up and Defragmentation

The best way of accessing these tools is by using **This PC** tile on the **Start** menu, locating the **C:** drive, touching and holding or right-clicking it, then selecting **Properties** from the displayed menu to open the screen in Fig. 11.6.

Fig. 11.6 The Properties Screen.

Tapping or clicking the **Disk Clean-up** button starts the utility. Selecting the **Tools** tab opens another dialogue box in which you can optimise the hard disc by rearranging its data to eliminate unused spaces, which speeds up access by all Windows and other program operations. Repeat both operations at least once a month.

Index